RETAIL MARKETING MANAGEMENT

Sara Miller McCune founded SAGE Publishing in 1965 to support the dissemination of usable knowledge and educate a global community. SAGE publishes more than 1000 journals and over 800 new books each year, spanning a wide range of subject areas. Our growing selection of library products includes archives, data, case studies and video. SAGE remains majority owned by our founder and after her lifetime will become owned by a charitable trust that secures the company's continued independence.

Los Angeles | London | New Delhi | Singapore | Washington DC | Melbourne

RETAIL MARKETING MANAGEMENT

The 5 Es of Retailing

Dhruv Grewal

Los Angeles | London | New Delhi
Singapore | Washington DC | Melbourne

Los Angeles | London | New Delhi
Singapore | Washington DC | Melbourne

SAGE Publications Ltd
1 Oliver's Yard
55 City Road
London EC1Y 1SP

SAGE Publications Inc.
2455 Teller Road
Thousand Oaks, California 91320

SAGE Publications India Pvt Ltd
B 1/I 1 Mohan Cooperative Industrial Area
Mathura Road
New Delhi 110 044

SAGE Publications Asia-Pacific Pte Ltd
3 Church Street
#10-04 Samsung Hub
Singapore 049483

Editor: Matthew Waters
Editorial assistant: Jasleen Kaur
Production editor: Martin Fox
Copyeditor: Christine Bitten
Proofreader: Derek Markham
Indexer: Silvia Benvenuto
Marketing manager: Alison Borg
Cover design: Francis Kenney
Typeset by: C&M Digitals (P) Ltd, Chennai, India
Printed in the UK by Bell & Bain Ltd, Glasgow

Library of Congress Control Number: 2018953094

British Library Cataloguing in Publication data

A catalogue record for this book is available from the British Library

ISBN 978-1-5264-4684-8
ISBN 978-1-5264-4685-5 (pbk)

At SAGE we take sustainability seriously. Most of our products are printed in the UK using responsibly sourced papers and boards. When we print overseas we ensure sustainable papers are used as measured by the PREPS grading system. We undertake an annual audit to monitor our sustainability.

To my uncle Indrajit Seth and aunt Jeet Seth

To my wife Diana Grewal, daughter Lauren Grewal, son-in-Law Chet Berman, son Alex Grewal, and Mother Saroj Grewal

CONTENTS

LIST OF FIGURES

LIST OF IMAGES

LIST OF TABLES

ABOUT THE AUTHOR

Dhruv Grewal (PhD, Virginia Tech) is the Toyota Chair in Commerce and Electronic Business and a Professor of Marketing at Babson College. His research and teaching interests focus on direct marketing and e-commerce, marketing research, the broad areas of value-based marketing strategies, services and retailing, and pricing. He is listed in *The World's Most Influential Scientific Minds*, Thompson Reuters, 2014 (only 8 from the marketing field and 95 from economics and business are listed). He is an Honorary Distinguished Visiting Professor of Retailing and Marketing, Center for Retailing, Stockholm School of Economics, an Honorary Distinguished Visiting Professor of Retailing and Marketing, Tecnologico de Monterrey, a GSBE Extramural Fellow, Maastricht University, a Global Chair in Marketing at University of Bath and has been a Visiting Scholar at Dartmouth. He has also served as a faculty member at the University of Miami, where he has also served as a department chair.

He was ranked 1st in the marketing field in terms of publications in the top six marketing journals during the 1991–1998 period and again for the 2000–2007 period and ranked 8th in terms of publications in *Journal of Marketing* and *Journal of Marketing Research* during the 2009–2013 period. He was also ranked 1st in terms of publications and 3rd in citations for pricing research for the time period 1980–2010 in 20 marketing and business publications. He has published over 150 journal articles in *Journal of Marketing, Journal of Consumer Research, Journal of Marketing Research, Journal of Retailing, Journal of Consumer Psychology, Journal of Applied Psychology,* and *Journal of the Academy of Marketing Science,* as well as many other journals. He has over 45,000 citations based on Google Scholar. He currently serves on numerous editorial review boards, such as *Journal of Marketing* (area editor), *Journal of the Academy of Marketing Science* (area editor), *Journal of Marketing Research* (associate editor), *Academy of Marketing Science Review, Journal of Interactive Marketing, Journal of Business Research* and *Journal of Public Policy & Marketing* and the advisory board for *Journal of Retailing.* He has also served on the boards of *Journal of Consumer Psychology* and *Journal of World Business.* He also received Best Reviewer Awards (*Journal of Retailing* 2008, *Journal of Marketing* 2014), Outstanding Area Editor (*Journal of Marketing* 2017, *Journal of the Academy of Marketing Science* 2016) and a Distinguished Service Award (*Journal of Retailing* 2009).

He was awarded the 2017 Robert B. Clarke Outstanding Educator Award (Marketing Edge, formerly DMEF), 2013 University wide Distinguished Graduate Alumnus from his alma mater Virginia Tech, the 2012 Lifetime Achievement Award in Pricing (American Marketing Association Retailing & Pricing SIG), the 2010 Lifetime Achievement Award in Retailing (American Marketing Association Retailing SIG), the 2005 Lifetime Achievement in Behavioral Pricing Award (Fordham University, November 2005) and the Academy of

Marketing Science Cutco/Vector Distinguished Educator Award in May 2010. He is a 'Distinguished Fellow' of the Academy of Marketing Science. He has served as VP Research and Conferences, American Marketing Association Academic Council (1999–2001) and as VP Development for the Academy of Marketing Science (2000–2002). He was co-editor of *Journal of Retailing* (2001–2007).

He has won a number of awards for his research: 2018 William R. Davidson *Journal of Retailing* Best Paper Award (for paper published in 2016), 2017 *Journal of Interactive Marketing* Best Paper Award (for paper published in 2016), 2016 *Journal of Marketing* Sheth Award, 2016 William R. Davidson *Journal of Retailing* Best Paper Award (for paper published in 2014), 2015 Luis W. Stern Award (American Marketing Association Interorganizational Sig), Babson College Faculty Scholarship Award (2015), William R. Davidson *Journal of Retailing* Best Paper Award 2012 (for paper published in 2010), 2011 Best Paper Award (La Londe Conference for Marketing Communications and Consumer Behavior), 2011 Luis W. Stern Award (American Marketing Association Interorganizational Sig), William R. Davidson *Journal of Retailing* Honorable Mention Award 2011 (for paper published in 2009), Babson College Faculty Scholarship Award (2010), William R. Davidson *Journal of Retailing* Best Paper Award 2010 (for paper published in 2008), William R. Davidson *Journal of Retailing* Honorable Mention Award 2010 (for paper published in 2008), 2017 Best Paper Award, Connecting for Good Track, Winter AMA Conference, Stanley C. Hollander Best Retailing Paper, Academy of Marketing Science Conference 2002, 2008 and 2016, M. Wayne DeLozier Best Conference Paper, Academy of Marketing Science 2002 and 2008, Best Paper, CB Track, Winter AMA 2009, Best Paper, Technology and e-Business Track, AMA Summer 2007, Best Paper Award, Pricing Track, Best Services Paper Award (2002), from the American Marketing Association Services SIG presented at the Service Frontier Conference, October 2003, Winter American Marketing Association Conference 2001, Best Paper Award, Technology Track, Summer American Marketing Association Educators' Conference 2000, and University of Miami School of Business Research Excellence Award for years 1991, 1995, 1996 and 1998. He has also been a finalist for the 2014 *Journal of Marketing* Harold H. Maynard Award, the 2012 Paul D. Converse Award, and the 2005 Best Services Paper Award from the Services SIG.

He has co-edited a number of special issues including: (Spring 1999) *Journal of Public Policy & Marketing* 'Pricing & Public Policy,' (Winter 2000) *Journal of the Academy of Marketing Science* 'Serving Customers and Consumers Effectively in the 21st Century: Emerging Issues and Solutions,' *Journal of Retailing* 'Creating and Delivering Value through Supply-Chain Management,' 2000, *Journal of Retailing*, 'Branding and Customer Loyalty 2004, *Journal of Retailing*, 'Service Excellence,' 2007, *Journal of Retailing*, 'Customer Experience Management,' 2009, and *Journal of Retailing*, 'Pricing in a Global Arena', 2012.

He co-chaired the 1993 Academy of Marketing Science Conference, the 1998 Winter American Marketing Association Conference 'Reflections and Future Directions for Marketing,' Marketing Science Institute Conference (December 1998) on 'Serving Customers and Consumers Effectively in the 21st Century: Emerging Issues and Solutions,' the 2001 AMA doctoral consortium, American Marketing Association 2006 Summer Educator's

Conference, 2008 Customer Experience Management Conference, 2010 Pricing Conference, 2011 DMEF research summit, 2012 AMA/ACRA First Triennial Retailing Conference, 2013 Pricing & Retailing Conferences, 2014 Shopper Marketing conference at SSE, and the 2015 AMA/ACRA Second Triennial Retailing Conference.

He has also coauthored *Marketing* (publisher McGraw-Hill, 1e 2008, 2e 2010 – awarded Revision of the Year, McGraw-Hill Corporate Achievement Award for Marketing, 2e with ConnectMarketing in the category of Content and Analytical Excellence, 3e 2012, 4e 2014, 5e 2016, 6e 2018), *M Series: Marketing* (publisher McGraw-Hill, 1e 2009, 2e 2011, 3e 2013, 4e 2015, 5e 2017, 6e 2019), *Retailing Management* (publisher McGraw-Hill, 9e 2014, 10e 2018 – it is the leading textbook in the field), and *Marketing Research* (publisher Houghton Mifflin, 1e 2004, 2e 2007). He was ranked #86 for Books in Business and Investing by Amazon (29 January 2013).

He has won many awards for his teaching: 2005 Sherwin-Williams Distinguished Teaching Award, Society for Marketing Advances, 2003 American Marketing Association, Award for Innovative Excellence in Marketing Education, 1999 Academy of Marketing Science Great Teachers in Marketing Award, Executive MBA Teaching Excellence Award (1998), School of Business Teaching Excellence Awards (1993, 1999), and Virginia Tech Certificate of Recognition for Outstanding Teaching (1989).

He has taught executive seminars/courses and/or worked on research projects with numerous firms, such as Dell, ExxonMobil, IRI, Radio Shack, Telcordia, Khimetrics, Profit-Logic, McKinsey, Ericsson, Motorola, Nextel, FP&L, Lucent, Sabre, Goodyear Tire & Rubber Company, Sherwin Williams, and Asahi. He has delivered seminars in US, Europe, Latin America, and Asia. He has served as an expert witness or worked as a consultant on numerous legal cases. He serves on the Board of Directors of Babson Global. He also served on the Board of Trustees of Marketing Edge.

ABOUT THE CONTRIBUTORS

Michael Levy, PhD (Ohio State University), is the Charles Clarke Reynolds Professor of Marketing Emeritus at Babson College. He received his PhD in business administration from The Ohio State University and his undergraduate and MS degrees in business administration from the University of Colorado at Boulder. He taught at Southern Methodist University before joining the faculty as professor and chair of the marketing department at the University of Miami. Professor Levy received the first ever Academic Lifetime Achievement Award presented at the 2015 AMA/ACRA Triennial Conference, '25 years of dedicated service to the Editorial Review Board of the Journal of Retailing,' (2011), McGraw-Hill Corporate Achievement Award for Grewal–Levy *Marketing* 2e with Connect in the Category of Excellence in Content and Analytics (2010), Revision of the Year for *Marketing* 2e (Grewal/Levy) from McGraw-Hill Irwin (2010), 2009 Lifetime Achievement Award, American Marketing Association, Retailing Special Interest Group (SIG) (at Summer AMA), Babson Faculty Scholarship Award (2009), and the Distinguished Service Award, *Journal of Retailing* (2009) (at Winter AMA). He was rated as one of the 'Best Researchers in Marketing,' in a survey published in *Marketing Educator* (Summer 1997). He has developed a strong stream of research in retailing, business logistics, financial retailing strategy, pricing, and sales management. He has published over 50 articles in leading marketing and logistics journals, including the *Journal of Retailing, Journal of Marketing, Journal of the Academy of Marketing Science*, and *Journal of Marketing Research*. He currently serves on the editorial review board of the *International Journal of Logistics Management, European Business Review*, and the Advisory Boards of *International Retailing and Marketing Review* and the *European Retail Research*. He is coauthor of *Retailing Management* (10e, 2018), which is the best-selling retailing text in the world; *Marketing* (5e, 2017) and *M-Marketing* (5e, 2018), all with McGraw-Hill Education. Professor Levy was co-editor of *Journal of Retailing* from 2001 to 2007. He co-chaired the 1993 Academy of Marketing Science conference and the 2006 Summer AMA conference. Professor Levy has worked in retailing and related disciplines throughout his professional life. Prior to his academic career, he worked for several retailers and a housewares distributor in Colorado. He has performed research projects with many retailers and retail technology firms, including Accenture, Federated Department Stores, Khimetrics (SAP), Mervyn's, Neiman Marcus, ProfitLogic (Oracle), Zale Corporation, and numerous law firms.

Britt Hackmann, Co-founder of Nubry.

PREFACE

Over the past three decades, my colleagues and I have studied a host of issues that we regarded as likely to drive both success and innovation in retailing. Through my research, teaching, and editorial roles, I have developed detailed ideas about how retailers innovate to appeal to consumers and achieve successful outcomes.

For example, I served as co-editor of *Journal of Retailing* from 2000 to 2007 – the oldest marketing journal still in existence, and second oldest business journal (after *Harvard Business Review*). During my editorship, my co-editor and I processed literally hundreds of manuscripts, and the insights they contained inevitably informed my own thoughts and understanding of retailing. Furthermore, I have actively spearheaded various thought-leadership conferences and journal special issues, in an explicit effort to learn and integrate insights from academics and practice. Many of these conferences and special issues highlighted and reinforced the critical need to explore the strategic side of retailing, through such an integration of academic research and practice (e.g., researchers interviewing leaders in various vertical markets and working with retailers to conduct field-based, real-world experiments). These foundations also underlie my previously published books, which similarly seek to bridge academic insights with practical realities, such as *Marketing*, *M: Marketing*, and *Retailing Management*.

For this text though, I wanted to add in something new. A book about innovative retailing needs to be innovative itself! Therefore, beyond the insights from academia and practice that have always informed my research, I decided to undertake extensive field-based research and also conduct a vast range of interviews with knowledgeable informants.

Accordingly, this text reflects contributions and discussions generously offered by members of the senior executive teams (e.g., chief marketing officers, chief executive officers, chief financial officers, chief operations officers, presidents, chief merchandise officers, heads of supply chains) of some of the world's most popular and successful retailers (e.g., CVS, Kroger, Zara, QuikTrip, ICA, Staples, BJs, Macy's, Ann Taylor, DSW, HSN). In addition, I solicited opinions and discussion with consultants who have worked with various firms on the cutting edge of retailing innovations (e.g., Dunnhumby, Accenture, McKinsey, Delliotte, IRI). The strategies outlined in this book reflect the companies' histories of successes and failures, as well as the lessons they have learned from them.

In that sense, the insights provided in the following pages reflect contributions from my own long research career, my extensive reading and editing of other scholars' contributions, interviews with practitioners performing actual retail innovations, and relevant insights from secondary sources when necessary. Collecting all these various sources prompted me to create the framework that guides this book. In turn, I hope the ideas shared in this book will help guide students and researchers working in the retailing or marketing fields – but I also hope that it proves useful and insightful for retail managers, service providers, and consulting firms. Even vendor managers for the firms that make up the retail supply chain – such as suppliers of consumer package goods, apparel or fashion brands, pharmaceutical manufacturers, and logistics providers – may benefit from applying the proposed frameworks and their related insights.

ACKNOWLEDGEMENTS

I deeply appreciate the insights shared by my collaborators, Michael Levy and Britt Hackmann, on certain chapters. I also acknowledge the help of Elisabeth Nevins, Scott Motyka, Carl-Philip Ahlbom, Lauren S. Grewal, Diana S. Grewal and Jenny Esdale. This book has benefited from my ongoing research collaborations – and literally hundreds of conversations – with my friends and colleagues: Anne L. Roggeveen, Victoria Crittenden, Anjali Bal, Lauren S. Beitelspacher, Krista Hill, Rajendra Sisodia, Thomas Davenport, Bala Iyer, Richard Hanna, Abdul Ali, and Ruth Gilleran (Babson College); Joan Lindsey-Mullikin (Cal Poly, San Luis Obispo); Ko de Ruyter (Kings College); Larry D. Compeau (Clarkson University); Praveen Kopalle and Kusum Ailawadi (Dartmouth); Rajneesh Suri (Drexel); Rajesh Chandrashekaran (Fairleigh Dickinson University); Gopal Iyer and Tamara Mangleburg (Florida Atlantic University); Anthony Miyazaki (Florida International University); Martin Mende and Maura Scott (Florida State University), Hooman Estelami (Fordham University); Ronnie Goodstein (Georgetown); V. Kumar (Georgia State University); Martin Wetzels and Dominik Mahr (Maastricht University); Yu Ma (McGill University); Maria Elena Vazquez Lira, Jan Meyer, and Eva M. González (Tecnológico de Monterrey); Lars Strannegård and Sara Rosengren (SSE) Zhen Zhu (Suffolk University); Venkatesh Shankar (Texas A&M); Dinesh Gauri (University of Arkansas); Veronica Hope Hailey, Brian Squire, Jens Nordfält Nancy M. Puccinelli and Elisa Schweiger (University of Bath); Arun Sharma, A. Parasuraman, R. Krishnan, Anuj Mehrotra, and Michael Tsiros (University of Miami); Francisco Villarroel Ordenes (University of Massachusetts Amherst); Stephan Ludwig (Surrey); Kent Monroe (University of Illinois); Abhijit Guha (University of South Carolina); Stephanie Noble (University of Tennessee); Rob Palmatier (University of Washington); Abhijit Biswas and Sujay Dutta (Wayne State University); and M. Joseph Sirgy (Virginia Tech).

I would also like to acknowledge the collaborations, connections and support provided by Hakon Swenson Foundation, Stockholm School of Economics, Maastricht University and University of Bath.

Finally, this book benefited from interactions and/or interviews with numerous retail practitioners: Claes-Göran Sylvén, Roland Fahlin, Per Strömberg, Fredrik Hägglund, Jonas Gunnarsson, Fredrik Holmvik, Caroline Berg, Tomas Axén, Gregg Mowins, Andy Volker, Kenneth Dickman, Tom Jacobsen, George Coleman, David Dillon, Don McGeorge, Don Becker, Linda Severin, Ted Sorozy, Bill Dankworth, Marnettee Perry, Simon Hay, Tom Gormley, Jesus Echevarria, Jose Martinez, Jevin Eagle, Ron Sargent, Don Ralph, Dona Rosenberg, Shira Goodman, Mike Miles, Don LeBlanc, Demos Parneros, Rob Price, Helena Faulkes, Dennis Palmer, Ramesh Murthy, Bari Harlam, Peter Amalfi, Tom Gallagher, Mike Atkinson, Steve Germain, Julie Sommers, Christine Neppl, Laura Sen, Christine Beauchamp, Mike Nicholson, Chet Cadieux, Bill Brand, Bryan Bradley, Julie Schmeling, Mindy Grossman, Rob Solomon, Carrie McDermott, Deborah Ferree, Doug Probst, Harris Mustafa, Kelly Cook, Mike MacDonald, Tim Adams, Karen Houget, Julie Griener, Ronnie Bindra, Mary Delk, Matt McNaghten, Julie Rusch and Leonard A. Schlesinger.

ONLINE RESOURCES

For Lecturers

Visit **https://study.sagepub.com/businessandmanagement** to access **PowerPoint slides** prepared by the author to support your teaching.

1

THE INNOVATIVE RETAILER

The modern retail landscape is dotted with vast opportunities but also is hedged in by extraordinary challenges. For every new and exciting retail channel, there is the looming threat of cannibalization and competition. The numerous innovative pricing schemes further increase the likelihood that customers will be trained to be more price sensitive. Each new product introduction promises thrilling success but is equally likely to end in crushing defeat. For every creative promotional idea, retailers face the threat of increased competition.

Once upon a time, retailing and many retailers were dominated by their buyers (and the buying organization). That is, to sustain satisfactory revenues, retailers had to buy their merchandise from suppliers more efficiently and smartly, negotiating deals that got them the best price. Then they could mark up their wares, display them on shelves, and wait for customers to show up to ensure their profits. As long as they sold appealing products, at a reasonable price, in a convenient location, with a few sales and promotions along the way, it seemed as if retailers could survive and thrive indefinitely. In truth, that perception was an illusion, and a majority of retailers – both well-established names and brand-new entrants – have embraced new ways of running their businesses to survive and thrive.[1]

In particular, online retailing has taken off. Amazon, with its more than \$170 billion in revenue, has been leading the way, though other actors, like Alibaba in China, have been steadily changing the retail landscape too. Consumers even have started to shift their online search practices, starting on Amazon when they begin looking for products, rather than typing a description into Google's search engine. To encourage such shifts, Amazon also is steadily integrating artificial intelligence (and Alexa) to prompt its customers to purchase more.[2]

If we acknowledge that the channels for conducting retail business have undergone dramatic change, then we also realize that the long-standing, well-known, widely accepted conventional view of business as defined by the 4Ps – place, price, product, and

Figure 1.1
Introducing the 5 Es:
entrepreneurial,
innovative and
customer-centric
mindset, excitement,
education, experience,
and engagement

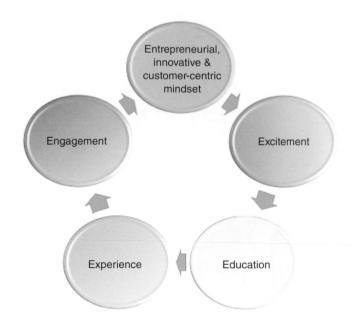

promotion – must be transformed. For retailers that want to innovate, change the game, remake the market, and establish themselves as the best in class, we suggest a new perspective, which is depicted in Figure 1.1.[3]

We offer innovative retailers, both today and in the future, a new framework for understanding how, where, and why they need to skillfully craft their strategies to ensure ongoing success. We offer a wealth of examples from leading retailers to reinforce our propositions and demonstrate the best practices, as well as corresponding actions these exemplars have taken to reach their stellar levels of success. By providing direct examples of retail movers and shakers (like Amazon), based on our years of research in this area, this book provides insights and ideas for emerging retailers, existing retailers, and students of retailing. In particular, this text aims to offer inspiration to those in the retail field who might find themselves limited to or stymied by their existing practices.

A Little Bit About …

Amazon[4]

When we start to talk about innovative retailers, it seems impossible to start anywhere else than with Amazon.com. The online retailing behemoth has been steadily growing over its entire history, such that it earns annual revenues of more than $170 billion. Its global reach and effective practices are evident and widely recognized; it has continually ranked as the top retailer in the American Customer Satisfaction Index (eight years in a row) and the UK Customer Satisfaction index (five years in a row). But even with this history of success, Amazon stringently avoids resting on its laurels and constantly seeks new retail innovations, as exemplified by three of its introductions that have changed the game for all retailers.

First, it was more than a decade ago that Prime launched, offering customers added benefits if they agreed to purchase an annual membership. The value of this offer has been clear enough that more than 100 million people have signed up, purchasing in excess of 5 billion items in a recent year. They received those items quickly and without shipping fees, such that Amazon totally reoriented consumers' expectations about when and how they could purchase items, in ways that were convenient, entertaining, and cost effective.

Second, many of those 5 billion items that shipped last year were Alexa devices. The in-home assistants allow consumers to access various products and services (e.g., music streaming, news updates). They also can link with approximately 4,000 smart home appliances, such that consumers, together with Alexa, are gaining an education in new ways to shop for everyday essentials.

Third, along with its technological advances, Amazon wants to engage constantly with its customers by being physically present where consumers are too. So it purchased Whole Foods, and it is experimenting with a new format of no-checkout stores, called Amazon Go. The purchase of Whole Foods prompted a novel experience, in that Prime members received special and exciting promotions in stores, as well as online. The product assortments also are innovative: Whole Foods' private-label brand 365 Everyday Value is now available through Amazon, Echo devices are appearing on shelves in Whole Foods stores, and consumers can even pick up their online purchases from Amazon Lockers in Whole Foods locations. Although the Amazon Go experiment is less expansive – so far, it has only opened one test location – the innovation manifested in a store that allows customers to grab their desired items and walk out without having to stand in line holds great promise. Shoppers who have experienced the store even call it 'magical.'

Outline of the Book

To help innovative managers and retail entrepreneurs pursue the path to success, we organize this book in five sections, in accordance with our 5E model. Thus, we begin where the best retailers begin: by devising and deriving an entrepreneurial mindset. In Chapter 2, we outline what defines an entrepreneurial retailer. In addition, we detail what differentiates entrepreneurs from dreamers – other than their success versus failure. True entrepreneurs take their gut feeling, dream, or crazy notion and confirm and further refine it based on market data, consumer feedback, research evidence, and any other relevant information they determine is necessary. Conversely, those who stay with their gut without taking that next step might believe they made their dream a reality when in fact they are simply joining the ranks of so many before them who consider the initial launch to be the end game – and fail miserably. Taking that final step of determining what else must be done and following through on it is vital to ongoing success. One of the executives we interviewed recalled an example of a company managed by merchandise visionaries, with great ideas but no operational orientation.[5] Without well-managed operations – that is, without determining just how, when, and where to interact and engage with every consumer segment – the retailer with great ideas will also be the one with declining sales.

The need for data, feedback, and information is particularly acute when it comes to achieving the second E in our framework: excitement. With Chapters 3 and 4, we offer retailers insights and ideas about how they can get the marketplace excited about their value propositions. In particular, we focus on the strategic use of store brands. Far from the generic, low quality image they once embodied, store brands have grown into the key means to differentiate one provider from the next and get customers excited to visit the store. A Pink lover knows that she can only get her beloved brand at Victoria's Secret, for example.

Furthermore, private labels are no longer a 'one-and-done' proposition. Whether we're dealing with Kroger, Tesco, or Zara, we highlight innovative retailers that offer a range of private-label brands, from high end to basic, from premium and organic to inexpensive and disposable. Such excitement is not limited to traditional stores either – more than 70 percent of the exciting offers from HSN are privately branded items.

But excitement can only accrue if consumers know what makes a game-changing retailer's offer so special. Education, the third E, implies that great retailers make sure their customers

Image 1.1
Victoria's Secret encourages customers to engage with the merchandise; their associates stand at the ready to help them with their needs

Source: Tooykrub / Shutterstock.com

know exactly how to gain the most value from their offerings. As we highlight in Chapters 5 and 6, education might involve a variety of activities like helping customers learn how to use a new channel, such as when Staples instructs in-store customers how they can purchase a desk that may be out of stock in the store at the time, yet available for delivery the next day, using an in-store kiosk that connects to the retailer's website. In other situations, education focuses mainly on the service offering. Great service is a byword of retail, but it only creates value and excites customers if those customers know it's available. For example, CVS informs loyal shoppers who already like this innovative retailer that its pharmacists will call them to make sure they are taking their medications correctly and on time. Such consumer-directed education activities enhance customers' engagement with the retailer.

Successful retailers are intentionally customer-centric, which is easy for small stores, where managers personally know each customer who walks in the door. Although it might seem that massive, international retailers cannot achieve this high level of customer-centricity, game-changing retailers have found ways to do so by managing the fourth E, that is, the shopping experience. In Chapter 7, we review how great retailers engineer the experience across shopping channels to ensure that a promise they make in person can be fulfilled consistently, regardless of the channel used. Managing the overall experience also requires sufficient inventory levels. At Zara, achieving this experiential aspect means equipping store managers with handheld devices that allow them to communicate continually in real-time with product developers and those in the procurement department.[6] It also requires keeping customers happy in their physical environment, which is why Kroger has instituted innovative policies to help customers avoid long checkout lines and thus ensure a pleasant experience for customers themselves, as well as for store employees.

Image 1.2
Self-service kiosks allow customers to gather information (education) and enhance their experience
Source: Carl-Philip Ahlbom

Ultimately, these four Es lead to the fifth and final E: engaging the customer. Engagement results in the customer remaining loyal to the retailer and satisfied with the offer. As Chapters 8 and 9 reveal, it is never enough to achieve engagement and then stop; it must be maintained consistently over time. Retail entrepreneurs who are changing the face of retailing harness the loyalty data that their excited, educated customers provide. Then they combine those data with precise retail analytics data. Accordingly, we offer a specific and detailed analysis of the 'analytical retailer' in Chapter 8, explicating how such innovators engage customers effectively. The insights they gather allow these entrepreneurs to initiate the 5E retail cycle all over again and in constant motion, ensuring that they keep pace with the ever-changing retail game.

A Detailed Introduction to the 5 Es

Before we get into examples and how the elements of this framework can be implemented, we want to make sure each aspect is perfectly clear. This chapter thus serves as not only an introduction to the book but also an introduction to how innovative retailers can reconsider their offerings, strategy, and methods according to the 5E framework.

Cultivating an Entrepreneurial, Innovative and Customer-centric Mindset

Traditionally, entrepreneurs have been defined by their efforts to initiate, organize, and operate new business ventures, which are inherently fraught with risk. Extensive research has focused explicitly on entrepreneurs and has detailed the various key qualities and requirements that such individuals must have. It also highlights the consistently high percentages of new ventures that fail – with some estimates in certain industries suggesting that as much as 90 percent of efforts fail within the first few years of their existence.

For this book though, we focus on innovative retailers. In Chapter 2, we reconceive of the entrepreneurial mindset as intimately and inherently associated with the connection that a retailer makes with its customers. It is therefore incumbent upon the retailer to devise an appropriate strategy that delivers a simple, straightforward, clear, and consistent message and offer that it shares with each and every potential and actual customer. Without the core competencies to accomplish this outcome, new retailers can never become true retail entrepreneurs, nor can they truly change the game.

Exciting the Customer through Value

To be exciting, the retail offering must provide value to customers. We adopt a market-based vision of value, as the relationship between what a customer gets for what she gives. An excited customer regards this trade-off as favorable for her situation, such that she would be willing to offer a little information about her preferences in return for a wealth of targeted, personalized product and service offerings. At Staples, the preferred customer account management program ensures that the customers who give the most, in terms of their spending, also get the most, in the form of optimized pricing on dozens of items.

When it comes to generating excitement, a well-integrated mix of modern communication and promotional tools can be very effective. But even the most cutting-edge retailers cannot afford to forget the fundamental demands of retail customers: having the right products in the right place at the right time. Chapter 3 addresses how innovative, game-changing retailers select from the proliferation of products available in nearly every industry, often by rationalizing their assortment. With a well-rationalized, appropriately localized assortment, the retailer makes sure that the right customers find exactly what they want (in-stock), when and where they want it, for a fair price.[7]

Of course, modern consumers have grown highly accustomed to finding what they want easily, because often their preferred product or service is just a mouse click or touchpad away. Such availability and the expanded use of promotions to excite customers means that the best retailers also design their pricing and promotional strategies with a particular eye toward creating value through excitement. The detailed analysis of massive amounts of data might seem like an odd notion to include in a chapter on excitement. One might wonder why the innovative retailers get so excited about massive data and spreadsheets, but by gathering, assessing, and applying lessons learned from their customer data, these retailers can make sure they remain consistently competitive in the prices they charge, products they offer, messages they communicate, and – of course – excitement they generate.

To reinforce an exciting value proposition, they also rely on promotions that are as varied as the many types of retailers. Whether using mass circulars, in-store events, gorgeous visual displays, targeted promotions, clearance sales – or combinations of some or all of these efforts – retail entrepreneurs make sure that value remains high, as do excitement levels.

One of the most effective routes to excitement these days is through a specific, proprietary store brand. Chapter 4 thus focuses wholly and specifically on this key element of the second E. In addition to outlining the history of store brands, we clarify how this trend plays out in modern retail. When the store *is* the brand, customers may get excited, but retailers also must appreciate the risk it could involve, so we also delve into the challenges associated with this aspect of the retail thrill ride.

Educating the Customer

By tailoring their educational activities for specific consumer segments, innovative retailers enhance the benefits they provide relative to the benefits that customers desire. For example, they use social media–based offers (e.g., mobile applications, games) to tell customers about their latest brand, product, idea, or outlet. Location-based software and mobile apps in particular can provide customers with information about a coupon, distinctive offer, or recommendation at the very moment they are making their purchase decision. As we discuss in Chapter 5, social networks provide excellent educational opportunities, as well as social connections. Through them, retailers can proactively inform millions of customers about the exciting deals they make available to consumers, such as a superlative Groupon price promotion.

Well-designed and orchestrated communications through various social media channels can draw customers through the various channels (online, mobile, brick and mortar) to take advantage of the calls to action. As consumers enter their websites or enter their stores, firms need to take advantage of these visits and educate the customer about their value proposition and use the opportunity to clearly communicate the benefits that are offered.[8] Some of this information may be new, but in other cases, education is all about reminding and reinforcing what people already know about a retail offering.

For example, customers might know already of a retailer's claim of offering superior service. But only if it continues educating and reminding them of this offering can a retailer be truly effective. In Chapter 6, we describe four paths that innovative retailers take to reach a 'service edge' that they can use to educate customers:

- Experience management.
- Value-added services.
- Store environmental control.
- Innovative solutions.

These four paths reflect specific combinations of revenue-generation and cost-management approaches. For example, if a retailer wants to generate more revenues from new operations, it devises appropriate value-added services, which in turn requires the development of methods for educating customers. If instead it needs to contain the costs of adding new operations, it likely seeks out different types of innovative solutions that enable it to do so. Retailers can deploy either revenue generation or cost containment to current operations or new ones. In either situation, it focuses on the customer's experience, whether in stores or not. Thus, it leads right into our next E.

Experiencing the Product or Service

YouTube has many entertaining vidoes on its website. However, the YouTube channel also serves as a valuable source of information about how various goods and services offered by retailers work and where they can be obtained. In this sense, one of the most popular websites in the world serves to simulate real experiences. Chapter 7 highlights in-store strategies that enhance such experiences, without ignoring how various channels can be used to mimic such experiences. Social media might be the latest and greatest innovation for retail strategy, but it still needs to provide a consistent, compelling experience that allows the retailer to acquire long-term, loyal customers. For example, Home Depot stores remain the primary source of information and instruction for do-it-yourselfers (DIYers). Additionally, Home Depot uses its website to communicate valuable information and instructions about the installation of a variety of products.

Image 1.3
Home Depot makes it possible for do-it-yourselfers to complete projects by educating them about the necessary tools and equipment, as well as giving them experience with practice projects

Source: Helen89 / Shutterstock.com

Engaging the Customer

Engaging with customers results in long-term relationships with them. These relationships engender loyalty, commitment, and greater profitability, because these customers are likely to purchase more products and services, and they are less expensive to engage with. In Chapter 8, loyalty is our main focus, including how loyalty programs encourage meaningful conversations with customers, push them up the 'loyalty ladder,' enable effective customer segmentation and strategic differentiation, and help reward a retailer's best customers. Although we offer multiple examples of innovative retailers that successfully engage customers in this chapter, we provide a particularly in-depth look at Kroger and its superlative loyalty program.

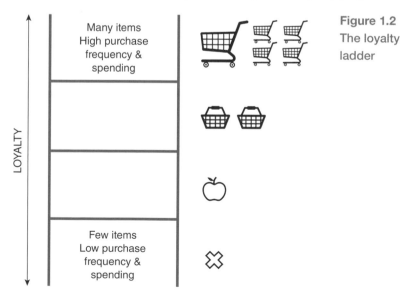

Figure 1.2
The loyalty ladder

Part of the reason Kroger fulfills the engagement demand so effectively is because of its extensive reliance on appropriate and insightful customer analytics. Customer-driven retail analytics, the topic of Chapter 9, integrate three main centers of activity: customers, the company (which includes formats, channels, stores, and employees), and strategic relationships (featuring both vendors and merchandise). An innovative, game-changing retailer creates and uses analytics systematically to guide and fine-tune its strategies. The strategy dedicated to each customer integrates the entire retail offering, from merchandise and marketing to supply chain and store operations, to achieve success.

TAKEAWAYS

- Innovative retailers excel on the 5E framework: entrepreneurial/innovative customer-centric leaders, excitement, education, experience, and engagement.
- This chapter provides a broad overview of the framework, as well as an introduction to the individual chapters that address each E in detail.

NOTES

1   Dhruv Grewal, Anne Roggeveen, and Jens Nordfält (2017) 'The Future of Retailing,' *Journal of Retailing*, 93, March, pp. 1–6; Dhruv Grewal, Anne L. Roggeveen, Rodney C. Runyan, Jens Nordfält, and Maria Elena Vazquez Lira (2017) 'Retailing in Today's World: Multiple Channels and Other Strategic Decisions Affecting Firm Performance,' *Journal of Retailing and Consumer Services*, 34, pp. 261–263; Interview with Kroger leadership team, such as Don McGeorge, former President and COO, Kroger.

2   Sapna Maheshwari (2017) 'As Amazon's Influence Grows, Marketers Scramble to Tailor Strategies,' *The New York Times,* 31 July; Jack Marshall (2017) 'Amazon Lures Publishers to New Social Network by Paying Them to Post,' *The Wall Street Journal*, 19 July; Lauren Johnson (2017) 'Amazon is Opening up its Ads Business, and Marketers See a Big Opportunity to Shake Up Search,' *AdWeek*, 13 September; 'Amazon Marketing Services,' available at: https://advertising.amazon.com/amazon-marketing-services (accessed 16 July 2018).

3   This framework builds on the 4E Model of Marketing. See Dhruv Grewal and Michael Levy (forthcoming), *Marketing*, 7th edn, New York: Mcgraw-Hill Education.

4   Jeffrey P. Bezos, 'Letter to Shareholders,' Amazon Annual Report 2017.

5   Interview with BJ's leadership team members such as Peter Amalfi, former Chief Information Officer, BJ's Wholesale Club.

6   Michael Levy, Barton A. Weitz, and Dhruv Grewal (2018) *Retailing Management*, 10th edn, Burr Ridge, IL: McGraw-Hill/Irwin; Dhruv Grewal, Michael Levy, R. Krishnan, and Jeanne Munger (2010) 'Retail Success and Key Drivers,' in Manfred

Krafft and Murali Mantrala (eds), *Retailing in the 21st Century: Current and Future Trends*, 2nd edn, New York: Springer Berlin Heidelberg, pp. 15–30. Also interview with Zara leadership members, such as Jesus Echevarria, communication officer.

7   Interview with Tom Gallagher, former Zone Vice President, BJ's Wholesale Club.

8   See Dhruv Grewal and Michael Levy (forthcoming), *Marketing*, 7th edn, New York: Mcgraw-Hill Education.

2

THE ENTREPRENEURIAL, INNOVATIVE, AND CUSTOMER-CENTRIC MINDSET

 **Text-specific Definition**

What is Entrepreneurship?

For this book, entrepreneurship refers to innovative leaders who connect with customers through their clear, consistent messages, which spread throughout the organization. This definition is a little different from traditional descriptions, because we believe that retail innovators stay entrepreneurial throughout their careers, not just when they are starting up a business.

Retailing leaders introduce a strategic skill set (and sometimes a little luck) in the right place at the right time to make the magic happen. Successful leaders are highly entrepreneurial and innovative by nature. Before a retail innovation can be successful, there must be some initial spark by a retail entrepreneur who creates (innovates) the idea, initiates the search for resources, and launches forth on the path. With apologies to the poet Robert Frost: To be able to forge the road less traveled, someone first needs to find the point where the two paths diverge. Then that innovative person can recruit strategic team members who share the vision and will produce a retail chain or a retail format that innovates to win.[1]

Innovative leaders offer the initial ideas or management styles that can transform the guiding vision of the retail firm. Our analysis is not limited to company founders though; a truly innovative leader can take an existing retailer and transform its vision to match his or her own. As we noted in the first chapter, we also go beyond this traditional view of entrepreneurs as people who start up and then operate new and risky business ventures. For this text, the retail innovator refers to those in the field who connect with customers by ensuring that their company delivers a simple, straightforward, clear, and consistent message. These retail innovators remain entrepreneurial throughout their careers, not just at the start.

Once in place, this innovative, entrepreneurial spirit can infuse the whole organization. It defines how the retailer conducts its overall business and connects with its stakeholders.[2] Such leaders tend to be charismatic and willing to take risks, though a discussion of leadership traits is a story for another book. It also is important to note early in this chapter that these innovative/entrepreneurial leaders do not create or transform the firm alone; rather, they have the strong drive and strength of vision to overcome the inherent resistance and inertia that marks virtually every organization.

Image 2.1
The proverbial road less travelled is a critical path for innovative entrepreneurs

Our goal here is to outline how innovative/entrepreneurial retail leaders take their vision and transform it into a strategy that ensures the retailer connects closely with each stakeholder, whether customers (both actual and potential), employees (top management and frontline, current and prospective), channel partners, or Wall Street.[3] Even when these leaders humbly minimize their own contributions, their top management team laud their praises and highlight how they stimulat the entire organization. We highlight five strategic elements consistently demonstrated by great innovative leaders:

1 Keep the strategy simple.
2 But make sure it is well developed too.
3 Then, keep the execution of this strategy consistent ...
4 By integrating it across all firm elements, and
5 Ensure that it is communicated to all audiences.

As the first E in our 5E framework, entrepreneurship might seem a little different, because it involves more than customers. Yet cutting-edge retailers either have or else obtain an ability to take the pulse of their customers and constantly adapt, innovate, and reinvent themselves. We split this chapter into five sections, to detail how new and existing retail entrepreneurs and managers can follow the lead of these game-changing innovators to make sure their companies connect with their stakeholders just as well.

Keep the Strategy Simple

The notion to 'keep it simple' is so widely used as to seem almost trivial. But for innovative retailers and their entrepreneurial leaders, the phrase rings true. The retail sector is filled with complications and details and distractions that can shift the strategic focus away from the central mission. Entrepreneurial leaders must establish a strategic vision that is not just straightforward and easy to understand but also specific and fitting for their innovative retail format or formats. The leader generally develops a strategic vision in conjunction with the management team.

Following through on the strategic vision, the leader, the management team, and the retailer market products and services that allow them to stay true to their shared vision.[4] Rather than spending time trying to mimic competitors or chasing customer whims, innovative retailers determine a strategy that works for them and stick with this overall value proposition. This is not to suggest that retail entrepreneurs never change; on the contrary, being nimble and dynamic might be an integral part of the central strategy for a great retailer. When the economy slowed down, retailers needed to react, but those innovative retailers with a simple strategy could do so more effectively by starting from an established foundation.[5]

A Little Bit About ...

Kroger[6]

Kroger Co. is one of the world's largest grocery retailers, with more than 2,700 stores in 35 states and annual sales of more than $120 billion. Its stores feature various formats, from grocery and department stores to discount and convenience stores to jewelry stores, functioning under approximately two dozen brand banners (e.g., Fred Meyer). Kroger stores carry up to 50,000 items, which vary from basic groceries to organic vegetables, natural foods, and hot meals. They also maintain more than 12,000 private-label items that account for about one-quarter of Kroger's total sales. Kroger produces approximately 40 percent of its private-label items at one of its more than 35 food processing plants. In addition, Kroger operates more than 2,200 in-store pharmacies and has installed gas pumps in nearly 1,200 locations. Its floral shops' sales make Kroger the world's largest florist too.

Barney Kroger opened his first store in 1883 in downtown Cincinnati, guided by the principals of service, selection, and value – similar to the notions that guide the company today. Kroger also has long embraced innovation: it was the first grocer in the United States to establish its own bakeries and sell both meats and groceries. It was also the first grocery chain to conduct consistent product quality inspections and scientifically test its foods; it accordingly won the 2012 Black Pearl Award from the International Association for Food Protection. In the 1970s, Kroger was the first grocery retailer to formalize consumer research and test electronic scanners. More recently, Kroger has pioneered the QueVision technology in an attempt to decrease checkout times. In terms of its sustainability efforts, in the mid-2000s, Kroger innovated a new process to cull safe, edible, fresh products that could not be sold and donate them promptly to local food banks.

Kroger is a company that has been quick to recognize when customer needs change and adapt accordingly. In so doing, it has not attempted to reinvent itself or change its strategy; instead, it has changed how it applies its consistent strategy.[7] The idea underlying 'keeping it simple' is that the entrepreneurial leader understands what makes the company unique and functional (i.e., the DNA of the firm), then lays out that strategy for the rest of the firm.[8] Accordingly, these leaders develop a simple strategy that is easy for employees to understand, connect with, follow through on, and feel proud to be a part of.[9]

In addition to the innovative retailers we interviewed (e.g., Kroger, CVS, HSN, ICA) that demonstrate such strategies and visions, other familiar illustrations include Nordstrom and Zappos.[10] They also include less familiar but emerging retailers such as Brandless, which appeared in a recent list of the most innovative companies. Its simple, straightforward premise is to offer approximately 250 nonperishable food and household items (i.e., groceries), without any brand names, connections, or images, each for $3.[11]

The prospects for Brandless, as a brand-new retail innovation, remain uncertain. But the example of Kroger, with its long history of success, might offer an example of how to maintain a simple strategy. Consider one pivotal 'Customer First' strategy for Kroger, communicated with a clear tag line: 'Earn loyalty for life.'[12] The strategy is simple in concept but still flexible and detailed enough to be meaningful. It articulates that Kroger devotes all its efforts, at every level, to encouraging customers to become loyal throughout their lifetimes, no matter their personal circumstances. Thus, if Kroger could identify a young couple just getting started, it would want to make sure it appealed enough to them that the household would continue shopping there as they added children, when those children left home, and they became empty nesters, whether they both worked, or one stayed home, and even well into their retirement years. Achieving such loyalty demands a consistency of purpose, to be what the customer needs at all times. It also involves the careful management of customers.[13]

Customer excellence is a hallmark of another retail chain, ICA Gruppen, a major Nordic retailer. Because it is imbued by a simple strategy, all stores in the chain, their managers, owners, and all employees understand and can effectively follow through on a central, strategic vision. Yet part of that vision is to personalize (or decentralize) according to location and store. That is, ICA is a huge group with a central idea of differentiating what it provides to customers. The CEO of ICA Gruppen recognizes that the strategic competitive advantage that the entrepreneurial owners of the chain's individual stores bring to the table is their passion for their local market and their business.[14] These talented owners and dedicated store managers and store employees focus on providing great value and service to the customers located in their area, in line with the overriding strategy of ensuring personalized service provision.

 **A Little Bit About ...**

ICA[15]

The innovative, diverse Nordic corporation ICA Gruppen dates back nearly a century. Since 1917, it has grown to over 2,100 stores, spanning Sweden, Norway, and the Baltic region, with annual sales of over SEK 100 billion (~US$11.8 billion). It employs more than 20,000 people in its grocery stores, as well as 50,000 or so in its offices, its logistics operations, or one of its own or retailer-owned stores in other industries. For example, ICA Bank earns the highest customer satisfaction

(Continued)

(Continued)

ranking in the region, while also reducing the cost of financial flows throughout ICA's diverse system. ICA Real Estate is one of the largest Nordic commercial real estate companies. ICA Gruppen also owns the Cervera, Hemtex, and inkClub brands. In 2014, ICA took the innovative step of rolling out online shopping in Sweden; it also has adopted a cutting-edge stance on sustainability by signing the Global Compact Caring for the Climate initiative and working with several nonprofit organizations, including the Red Cross and World Wildlife Federation.[16]

A simple but elegant, comprehensive retail strategy in turn should inform all strategic decisions, location choices, advertising methods, target markets, and pricing choices.[16] It is crucial that a retailer understands what it wants to be and then goes about communicating this strategy in a simple, straightforward fashion.[17] At Staples for example, the strategy of being 'easy' for customers means that it includes a delivery option in every sales channel, so that small business owners never have to leave their busy (often home-based) offices. A large part of its 'more easy' strategy and early success stems from Staples' successful integration of its multiple channels (catalogue, online, and stores) and ability to provide a vast range of products and services online. Yet even this exemplar has faced more difficulties in recent times, largely due to competition from online retailers like Amazon.[18]

But Make Sure It Is Well Developed Too

Simplicity does not mean weak or insufficient; it means easy to understand. But part of comprehension is ensuring that the idea or concept is well enough developed and defined that there can be no confusion. When a retailer like Kroger says its goal is customer loyalty for life or Staples wants to make things easy for its customers, each retailer must in parallel make sure that its strategy supports efforts to achieve that result.

To cultivate this strong strategic development throughout the firm, the leader needs to understand all aspects of the business and carefully formulate and communicate the strategy to all levels.[19] At the start of this century, Kroger undertook a strategic analysis of the grocery industry and its place in it to determine where the company was, where it needed to go, and how to get there. In particular, its innovative leaders realized that because the grocery industry was undergoing changes in response to new and altered customer demands, the retailer needed to adjust too, if it were going to succeed. Such efforts represent a hallmark of innovative leadership.

David Dillon served as the CEO of Kroger from 2003–2014, during which time Kroger and its management team created the 'Customer First' strategy that would enable the whole organization, more than 2,500 stores and 300,000 employees – from the top management team to workers on the retail floor – to communicate and execute it consistently.[20] As recounted by

Dillon, this strategic shift led Kroger to develop four key pillars, reflecting the four responses that it sought to invoke among every person who shopped in its stores:

1   The employees here are great.
2   The prices are reasonable (i.e., both low enough and justifiable).
3   All the products I want are here, plus a little something extra.
4   I want to return to have a similar shopping experience in the future.

As a result of its careful analysis and assessment – and then its effective development of a simple, clear-cut, four-pillar strategy – Kroger found that the global recession was less of a concern for it than it proved to be for many retailers. Even in a tough economy retailers faced unprecedented challenges, Kroger could stay the course with its foundational strategies, which reflected its in-depth understanding of what customers wanted and how it could deliver on those desires with its employees, prices, products, and shopping environment.

Kroger also partnered with the marketing research firm Dunnhumby, creating Dunnhumby USA, to realize a key element of the 'Customer First' strategy: pursuing an in-depth understanding of the needs of its customers. (We describe this partnership in more detail in Chapter 8.) Kroger thus gained access to the most advanced, sophisticated analytics to further understand and better serve its customers' needs.[21] As a result, Kroger's top managers could readily gather extensive and detailed information about its customers and integrate it into its simple strategy. Consequently, it developed a clear plan for connecting with customers by creating unique incentives and promotions for customers, selecting an appropriate assortment, and enhancing the assortment with store brands.

Then, Keep the Execution of the Strategy Consistent …

Innovative retailers understand that decisions about how to implement a particular strategy are ongoing and must be consistently managed over a period of time, in alignment with the strategy. The strategy is not just the vision of the entrepreneurial leader or CEO; it must be shared by the management team and all store employees, then implemented accordingly.[22] In retailing, an important but relevant phrase is 'retail is detail.' This phrase, a hallmark of retail success, highlights the importance of consistent execution of the strategy.

When Mindy Grossman arrived at HSN as its CEO in 2006 (her tenure lasted until 2017), she recognized both what worked and what didn't for the television-oriented retailer. She took this pioneer of electronic retailing and worked with her management team to transform it into a lifestyle network that ensures that customers' experiences are consistent, seamless, and excellent across the various channels.

In 2016, HSN earned retail revenues of more than $3 billion.[23] In implementing its strategy, HSN clearly understood the underlying importance of the customer experience and the need for HSN's execution of its strategy to be consistent across all its channels.[24] Thus, though Grossman retained HSN's entrepreneurial culture, within a year of taking over, she had transformed and steadily changed every aspect of the 30-year-old, linear television retailer into a lifestyle network and brand. Under her leadership, HSN adjusted nearly every element: merchandise, brands, personalities, customer service, and e-commerce, to name just a few. It also incorporated new and visionary innovations, such as Shop by Remote and HSN Live. Since that time, HSN has been acquired by QVC (its main competitor), in an ongoing effort to combat Amazon. Together, they represent one of the largest e-commerce retailers in the world.[25]

 **A Little Bit About ...**

HSN[26]

HSN Inc. is a $3.5 billion, innovative, direct-to-customer entertainment and lifestyle retailer that consists of two main components: HSN and Cornerstone. Since starting in St. Petersburg, Florida, in 1981, HSN has grown to encompass 6,700 employees. It broadcasts live to 90 million homes. HSN features both exclusive private labels and name brand products. Along with its television channel and catalogs, HSN engages customers digitally; it is currently the only retailer to offer live video streaming, 24 hours a day, through television, online, a mobile app, and the website. Its innovative Shop by Remote service has no parallel. The Cornerstone segment of HSN includes a vast catalog operation that distributes more than 280 million catalogs annually, maintains eight separate websites, and runs 16 brick-and-mortar retail and outlet stores. Cornerstone is better known by is multiple, prominent brands: Ballard Designs, Chasing Fireflies, Frontgate, Garnet Hill, Grandin Road, Improvements, and TravelSmith.

These changes highlight the powerful influence of this entrepreneurial leader. She brought in her vision and, within a year, had transformed HSN's strategy, while also retaining the elements that differentiated it from competitors and made it something special. Furthermore, Grossman was confident enough in her leadership that HSN undertook this massive shift while also contending with the most extensive global economic recession in modern history – a time when virtually all its competitors were shrinking away from taking on new initiatives. But in line with HSN's entrepreneurial strategy and Grossman's entrepreneurial leadership, it executed on its plan. The top management team also believed that the key to the firm's success was the continual, consistent execution of its strong business and brand strategies.[27] These strong and consistent applications of a strategy, throughout the organization, also require building a management team that shares the leader's vision, as well as the responsibility for buy-in and execution of the strategy. Thus, even after Grossman left to become the CEO of Weight Watchers, the strategy at HSN remained in place, reflecting the broad managerial support for that vision.

By Integrating it Across All Elements, and

When the simple, consistent strategy permeates every aspect of the organization, it becomes part of the retailer's very image. Innovative retailers carve out their space by defining and then implementing their strategy in every channel, at every touchpoint, through every level of customer contact. For example, if we were to conduct a survey of consumers in the United States, asking them to engage in free association and identify the retailer associated with certain value propositions, we would likely find that low prices are associated with Walmart, an online presence links with Amazon, and notions of quality arise when people think about Target. The following word clouds affirm this prediction; they came from a recent survey of what people thought of when presented with each retail brand.[28]

In its efforts to encourage shoppers to think 'easy' when they thought of Staples, the retailer promoted the 'Easy Button' not just as a gimmick for advertisements but also as a defining element of its strategy and a constant visual reminder of both its strategy and its brand promise.[29] It spans every aspect of the firm, from delivery (e.g., right merchandise delivered on time), to in-store (e.g., available products, easy to check out) and online (e.g., easy to order and next-day-delivery for free).[30]

Figure 2.1
Amazon word map

Source: Dinesh Gauri

Figure 2.2
Walmart word
map

Source: Dinesh
Gauri

Figure 2.3
Target word map

Source: Dinesh
Gauri

Similarly, HSN's seamless integration across multiple channels (television, online, mobile, catalog) reflects its strategy to provide customers with outstanding products and experiences, which means stellar customer service across the board, from the hosts featured on television to the person filling orders in the call center. To achieve this consistency, the organization ensures that the strategic vision (and intent) is clear.[31]

Ensure That It Is Communicated to All Audiences

A strategy can be effective only when the relevant stakeholders know what it is. Innovative retail leaders constantly work to express their expectations and simple, consistent strategy to everyone with whom they come into contact, from fellow members of the management team to employees to customers to channel partners. At Kroger, the 'Customer First' strategy thus became part of its daily DNA.[32]

An innovative retailer understands that the way a strategy is communicated must be tailored to be meaningful to different stakeholder groups and resonate with them through different channels. For example, DSW maintains a consistent and simple strategy, but it describes it in somewhat different terms for its various audiences. For investors, the corporate website notes:

> Our core focus is to create a distinctive shopping experience that satisfies both the rational and emotional shopping needs of our DSW customers by offering them a vast, exciting assortment of in-season styles combined with the convenience and value they desire.[33]

The message on the same site but a different page, targeted more toward consumers and casual browsers, still focuses on the same topics, but with a much less formal approach and more fun language:

> DSW is all about the thrill of finding the perfect shoe at the perfect price. A huge assortment of handbags and accessories also adds to the breathtaking assortment DSW is known for. For an even bigger selection, Shoe Lovers can shop anytime at dsw.com (where kids' shoes are ready and waiting!), making it crazy-convenient to explore all the fashion that DSW has to offer. To top it all off, DSW Rewards means shopping comes with perks.[34]

Because innovative retailing involves communicating a consistent strategy distinctively for each group that interacts with the firm – whether top management, employees, channel partners, or customers – we detail each stakeholder separately in this section, along with key examples of the types of communication that can lead to innovative retail success.

Top Management Team

When a new leader comes in to change the game, interactions with the top management team can remain a challenge, assuming that some of the members remain from before the transformation. How can an innovative leader convince the C-suite that her new way will change the game for the better?

The key is ensuring that other top managers know exactly what the strategy is and their role in implementing it. An entrepreneurial leader makes a concerted effort to ensure that the next level of management knows exactly what is expected, when and how, as well as how those expectations relate to the firm's overall strategy.[35] By repeating the message over and over again, using the terminology adopted throughout the implementation of the strategy, a retail head can get everyone at the top on the same innovative path.

Employees

Much of the responsibility granted to the top management team involves finding ways to communicate the strategy effectively to the people in their departments. In retail settings, frontline sales and service personnel invariably are central to implementing a game-changing retail strategy. Kroger tries to keep things simple by consistently citing its four key strategic pillars and putting the customer first (as we described in the previous section on integrating the strategy across elements). By narrowing down sales and service staff responsibilities to four key pillars, this innovative retailer seeks to ensure that everyone – filling every capacity, from newly hired stock clerks to store managers who have been with the company for decades – can state confidently what their role is in making sure that Kroger puts the customer first. For example, they know that their daily actions are the primary determinant of whether customers think the people at Kroger are great – the first key. They understand that getting the product mix right requires them to order the right items, then stock them quickly and accurately – the third key. According to our informants, employees know exactly how to help connect to that straightforward, clear, and simple strategy, because the four keys are communicated, over and over again. All these communications support the message that the customer must come first at Kroger.

Channel Partners

For DSW, transforming from a cheap source of shoes with moderate quality into a viable competitor in a broader landscape required a revision to the previous strategy. The goal was to ensure the retailer would become a viable destination for fashionable shoppers. Therefore, when a new, innovative leader arrived, the retailer made sure that it shared its new vision, strategy, and business model with every core vendor, to ensure that they were all in-sync and honest with one another.[36]

Such a strategic approach is not all that uncommon. In the office supply market for example, many retailers 'beat up' their suppliers, seeking to gain the best prices. They can do so because the office giants are international in their scope, so they dominate the retail channel; it is essential for a manufacturer of ink cartridges, for example, to have a presence on big box shelves. Yet for innovative retailers, such channel dominance is no longer the best route. Instead, at Staples, the preferred approach is to identify strategic suppliers whose representatives will meet with the executive team, share their strategy, and embrace the importance of a joint, shared vision.[37] Not only is Staples consistent in its strategy, but it also treats its vendors as true partners, by paying vendor invoices on time and working hard to maintain its reputation for fair dealing across the board.

More and more retailers also are working to increase efficiencies and minimize cost structures by adopting robotic technology in their distribution centers. Technology-forward retail innovators, such as Amazon and Alibaba, are particularly active in developing such novel supply chain operations and already rely heavily on robots to improve the delivery process, with promises of further uses as well (e.g., drones, self-driving delivery trucks). In brick-and-mortar locations maintained by retailers such as Walmart, robots are also being used to stock items and provide basic services and information to customers.[38]

Customers

We've saved perhaps the most important for last. If customers do not know or cannot perceive at least the outcomes of a firm's basic strategy, the strategy will fail. Consider examples of how the innovative retailers we have presented thus far in the chapter address consumers:

- On its customer website, DSW uses fun, informal language and fashionable graphics to establish itself as the prime source of the most exciting and compelling footwear available.
- For BJ's, value is the catchword. Many consumers may assume BJ's is not the place for them, perhaps because they have small families or prefer more organic options. To overcome such views, BJ's works hard to educate consumers and reinforce its identity and value.[39]
- When HSN revised its strategy with the arrival of its new CEO, it recognized that communicating this strategy represented a form of storytelling, in which the products were the main characters.[40] In whatever way it communicates with customers – television, online, call centers – the story remains the same.
- Kroger's communication is all about its four keys for putting the customer first. It's just that simple.

Conclusion

Recall from the previous chapter that we contrasted a traditional definition of entrepreneurs – as those people who initiate, organize, and operate new business ventures, which are inherently fraught with risk – against our view of the retail innovator, who connects with customers by ensuring that her company delivers a simple, straightforward, clear, and consistent message.

As this chapter reveals, some retail innovators embody this view of entrepreneurship throughout their organizations. This first E in our 5E framework sits apart from the other four, in that it might not appear, at first glance, to be directed specifically at customers. But as this chapter has shown, regardless of the strategy they use, entrepreneurial, innovative retailers keep it simple, develop it well, keep it consistent, integrate it everywhere, and communicate it to everyone.

With these five efforts, innovative and entrepreneurial retail leaders also achieve the objective that is central for anyone engaged in any sort of transaction: value. That is, the steps they take and the way they communicate ensure that the retail offering has value for customers. Such value can be effectively described by the next E in our framework. We're talking about excitement through value and what it means for innovative retailers. Please turn to the next chapter to find out what we mean.

TAKEAWAYS

- Regardless of the strategy they use, entrepreneurial, innovative retailers keep it simple, develop it well, keep it consistent, integrate it everywhere, and communicate it to everyone.
- Innovative retailers are entrepreneurial, but not just in a conventional sense. They constantly seek ways to connect with customers, embracing an entrepreneurial spirit even if they run well-established, well-known, long-standing organizations.
- They also establish this entrepreneurial spirit throughout their organizations, ensuring that this first E persists, even if they take other roles.

NOTES

1 Interview with HSN leadership team including Mindy Grossman, former CEO, HSN.
2 Interview with HSN leadership team including Judy Schmeling, former COO and CFO, HSN.
3 The role of entrepreneurial orientation is well documented in entrepreneurship, marketing, and strategy literature. Rauch et al. (2009, p. 762) highlight that an entrepreneurial orientation incorporates 'strategy-making processes that provide organizations with a basis for entrepreneurial decisions and actions.' See Andreas Rauch, Johan Wiklund, G.T. Lumpkin, and Michael Frese (2009) 'Entrepreneurial Orientation and Business Performance: An Assessment of Past Research and Suggestions for the Future,' *Entrepreneurship Theory and Practice,* 33, pp. 761–787. A further review is available in Dhruv Grewal, Gopalkrishnan Iyer, Rajshekhar G. Javalgi, and Lori Radulovich (2011) 'Franchise Partnership and International Expansion: A Conceptual Framework and Research Propositions,' *Entrepreneurial Theory and Practice*, May, pp. 533–557.
4 Interview with Kroger leadership team including David Dillon, former CEO and Chairman of the Board, Kroger.
5 A good example of how retailers changed their strategy to deal with rising gas prices is highlighted in Yu May, Kusum L. Ailawadi, Dinesh Gauri, and Dhruv Grewal

(2011) 'An Empirical Investigation of the Impact of Gasoline Prices on Grocery Shopping Behavior,' *Journal of Marketing*, 75, pp. 18–35.

6   See 'About Kroger,' available at: www.thekrogerco.com/about-kroger (accessed 17 July 2018).

7   Interview with Dillon, Kroger.

8   Arthur Thompson, Margaret Peteraf, John Gamble, and Alonzo J. Strickland III (2013) *Crafting & Executing Strategy: The Quest for Competitive Advantage: Concepts and Cases*, 19th edn, New York: McGraw-Hill Education.

9   Interview with Don McGeorge, Former President and COO Kroger.

10 Robert Spector and Patrick D. McCarthy (2005) *The Nordstrom Way to Customer Service Excellence: A Handbook for Implementing Great Service in Your Organization*, New York: John Wiley & Sons; Tony Hsieh (2010) *Delivering Happiness: A Path to Profits, Passion, and Purpose*, New York: Hachette Digital, Inc.; Tony Hsieh (2010) 'Zappos's CEO on Going to Extremes for Customers,' *Harvard Business Review*, 88(7), pp. 41–45.

11 Brandless (see: https://brandless.com); 'The World's Most Innovative Companies 2018,' *Fast Company*, available at: www.fastcompany.com/company/brandless (accessed 17 July 2018).

12 Interview with Ted Sarosy, former Vice President, Customer Loyalty and Interactive Marketing, Kroger; see also 'Kroger's Customer First Delivers Strong Sales, Loyalty,' *Retail Info Systems News*, 22 June 2010, available at: http://risnews.edgl.com/retail-news/Kroger-s-Customer-First-Delivers-Strong-Sales,-Loyalty37738 (accessed 17 July 2018).

13 For an excellent discussion on managing customers, see two books by V. Kumar: *Managing Customers for Profit: Strategies to Increase Profits and Build Loyalty*, Upper Saddle River, NJ: Pearson, 2008; and *Customer Relationship Management*, 2nd edn, New York: John Wiley & Sons, 2012.

14 Interview with Per Strömberg, CEO, ICA Gruppen.

15 ICA Gruppen, Annual Reports 2016, 2017, available at: www.icagruppen.se/en/rapportportal/annual-report-2016/ (accessed 17 July 2018); www.icagruppen.se/en/ (accessed 17 July 2018).

16 Michael Levy, Barton A. Weitz, and Dhruv Grewal (2018) *Retailing Management*, 10th edn, New York: McGraw-Hill Education.

17 Interview with Andrew Voelker, Former Senior Manager, Accenture; Interview with Ken Dickman, former Partner, Accenture.

18 Zachs Equity Research (2018) 'Staples (SPLS) Q2 Earnings Meet, Revenues Beat Estimates,' 24 August, available at: www.nasdaq.com/article/staples-spls-q2-earnings-meet-revenues-beat-estimates-cm836582 (accessed 17 July 2018).

19 Interview with Tom Gormley, former Senior Vice President, Dunnhumby USA.

20 Interview with Dillon, Kroger; see also www.kroger.com

21   Rajkumar Venkatesan and Paul W. Farris (2011) 'The End of Irrelevance: Dunnhumy's Best Customer Communications,' case study, University of Virginia, 29 June, GBUS8630.

22   David L. Bradford and Allan R. Cohen (1998) *Power Up: Transforming Organizations Through Shared Leadership*, New York: John Wiley & Sons.

23   Interview with Grossman, HSN; and also Mindy Grossman bio.

24   The importance of understanding the customer experience and managing it has been highlighted in retailing literature. See Dhruv Grewal, Michael Levy, and V. Kumar (2009) 'Customer Experience Management: An Organizing Framework,' *Journal of Retailing*, 85(1), pp. 1–14; Nancy Puccinelli, Ronald C. Goodstein, Dhruv Grewal, Rob Price, Priya Raghubir, and David Stewart (2009) 'Customer Experience Management in Retailing: Understanding the Buying Process,' *Journal of Retailing*, 85(1), pp. 15–30.

25   Phil Wahba (2017) 'QVC's $2.1 Billion Bet on HSN is a Move to Fight Amazon,' *Fortune*, 6 July, available at: http://fortune.com/2017/07/06/qvc-hsn/ (accessed 17 July 2018).

26   See: www.hsni.com/ (accessed 17 July 2018); HSN Inc., Form 10-K, 2016, available at: www.annualreports.com/Company/hsn-inc (accessed 17 July 2018).

27   Interview with Grossman, HSN.

28   Dinesh Gauri (2018) 'Shopping Habits and Retailer Perceptions: A Research Study,' Walton College of Business, University of Arkansas.

29   Interview with Shira Goodman, former President, North American Commercial, Staples; Interview with Michael Miles, former President and COO, Staples; Interview with Ronald Sargent, Staples.

30   Interview with Goodman, Staples; Interview with Miles, Staples; Interview with Sargent, Staples.

31   Interview with Rob Solomon, former Executive Vice President, Customer Care and Operations Administration, HSN.

32   Interview with McGregor, Kroger.

33   Interview with Kelly Cook, former EVP and Chief Marketing Officer, DSW; see also DSW, 'Company Profile,' available at: http://investors.dswshoe.com/ (accessed 17 July 2018).

34   DSW, 'About Us,' available at: www.dswinc.com/about_dsw.jsp (accessed 17 July 2018).

35   See Michael E. Porter, Jay W. Lorsch, and Nitin Nohria (2004) 'Seven Surprises for New CEOs,' *Harvard Business Review*, October, available at: https://hbr.org/2004/10/seven-surprises-for-new-ceos (accessed 17 July 2018); Susan Tardanico (2012) '5 Habits of Highly Effective Communicators,' *Forbes*, 29 November, available at: www.forbes.com/sites/susantardanico/2012/11/29/5-habits-of-highly-effective-communicators/ (accessed 17 July 2018).

36 Interview with Deborah Ferree, Vice Chairman and Chief Merchandising Officer, DSW.

37 Interview with Jevin Eagle, former Executive Vice President, Merchandising and Marketing, Staples; Interview with Don Ralph, SVP Supply Chain & Logistics, Staples.

38 Cate Trotter (2018) '45 Top Retail Innovations from NRF 2018 Innovation Lab,' *Insider Trends*, 8 February; Tomio Geron (2017) 'Driverless Trucks are Barreling Ahead,' *The Wall Street Journal*, 27 July; Sarah Nassauer (2016) 'Robots are Replacing Workers Where you Shop,' *The Wall Street Journal*, 19 July; Brian Baskin (2017) 'Next Leap for Robots: Picking Out and Boxing Your Online Order,' *The Wall Street Journal*, 25 July; George Anderson (2017) 'Walmart Puts Robots to Work with Humans in More Stores,' *Retail Wire*, 27 October.

39 Interviews with members of BJ's leadership team.

40 Bridget McCrea (2014) 'Mobilizing the Home Shopping Space,' *Response Magazine*, June, pp. 39–41.

3

VALUE
CREATES
EXCITEMENT

 Text-specific Definition

What is Excitement?

Innovative retailers get customers excited by what they offer, including when and where it is available and how it is priced. By combining these factors effectively, innovative retailers provide customers with value, and that's often the most exciting thing a shopper can encounter.

Regardless of what they sell, innovative retailers get customers excited by offering some form of stellar, thrilling value. Whether they offer grocery staples or installation services, socks or couture, shows or designer bags, retailers need to ensure that all their efforts ultimately give customers what they want, when they want it, and for a price they consider appropriate. The right combination gives any shopper a thrill.

In this chapter, we further build on our discussion from Chapter 2 about the importance of building on a leader's strategic vision to include how to enhance excitement to create value. We identify some key decisions (depicted in Figure 3.1) that innovative retailing leaders and their management teams must address:

1   What merchandise assortment to carry (and what not to carry) to attract consumers into a store or to a retailer's website and to entice them to make a purchase.
2   When and where to allocate merchandise across stores in different regions and appropriately place items in stores to make customers feel as if they need a specific product at that exact place and time.
3   How to price the merchandise to achieve acceptable margins while exciting customers with the great value offerings.

Every retailer wrestles with understanding how customers perceive 'value,' struggling to create excitement through this understanding. It involves trading off what merchandise is carried, along with where and when it is allocated, against how it is priced. Achieving this trade-off is a little like constantly adding to and taking things off a scale; on one side is the merchandise being offered, and on the other is the price charged for the merchandise. Merchandise, assortment, and pricing decisions can make or break a retailer – as innumerable examples of failed experiments show us.

But we focus instead on those that succeed – that is, on how innovative retailers make merchandise decisions that reflect consumer needs, based on insights gleaned from their cumulative experience, data, and built-in analytics. With its more than 25,000 stock keeping units (SKUs) in over 500 stores, DSW recognizes that merchandising is a key part of its business model, for example.[1]

Figure 3.1
The elements of exciting value

Merchandise Selection and Retention: The 'What'

Innovative retailers carefully use a combination of their customer loyalty data, data from manufacturers, and traditional marketing research data to select the precise merchandise that they will carry. Some of these decisions relate to striking a balance between the national and store brands that they carry (covered in more detail in Chapter 4). But a broader question relates to how much: how much to carry overall, how much in each product category, how much in each line, and even how much of each size, design, flavor, or color combination.

Therefore, as we detail in this section, the 'what' function for exciting value comprises three sub-decisions:

1   Defining what products mean to customers.
2   Adding exciting products.
3   Removing unexciting products.

To heighten customers' excitement and appeal to broad customer groups, many retailers focus on increasing the variety of merchandise they offer, because customers for decades have consistently ranked variety as one of the most important factors in their shopping decisions.[2] Greater variety in stores gives customers a fun, one-stop shopping experience, evoking an emotional sense of excitement. When these customers also appreciate the convenience of making multiple, often disparate purchases under one roof, wide variety grants them a more practical form of excitement (e.g., 'I finished all my shopping in one trip – now I can cross all of those tasks off my to-do list!'). Kroger has added a private-label fashion brand, 'Our Brand,' in the hope of becoming a go-to source of more than just pantry staples. Beyond an initial rollout of the newly designed clothing lines at 300 of its US stores, it hopes to incorporate fashion into its more than 2,700 locations in the future.[3] At the Wellery (a temporary pop-up gym), housed within Saks Fifth Avenue's flagship store in New York City, customers tested out the gym equipment, took fitness classes, and received massages. Saks hoped the offerings provided customers with a new way to feel good while they were in the store, as a means of encouraging more frequent visits. If customers happened to pick up a new pair of yoga pants on the way out, well then, even better.[4] Many retailers' expanded offerings even include various services (e.g., cafés in stores) to provide customers 'more reasons ... to come more often.'[5]

Broadening in-store assortments is a matter of balance, however, because it can create another threat for retailers, both online and in brick-and-mortar channels. That is, a vast assortment might draw customers and increase the retailer's share of the customers' wallet, but it also dilutes the retailer's identity, making it less clear what the retailer is known for, and therefore why customers should shop there. Inventory carrying costs increase too, in the form of investment costs and space, storage, and handling costs. Moreover, the more types of merchandise it carries, the more the retailer competes with different types of other retailers. Finally, brick-and-mortar stores have the additional constraint of limited space, so when faced with decisions about broadening assortments, managers must respond only after careful consideration of the consequences.

Managing the Assortment: What Do Products Mean to Customers?

Managing an assortment effectively starts with an understanding of what each product means to customers. Several key factors (penetration, sales, exclusivity) should be considered in developing this understanding. The *penetration* of an SKU is the market share of the product within its category. *Sales* refer to the metric the store uses to calculate sales levels for that product. *Exclusivity* is the extent to which consumers can purchase a substitute for a particular product.

Kroger uses these three factors to define nine 'MyLife' segments (e.g., 'Watching the Waistline,' 'Shoppers on a Budget,' 'Finest Households') of customers, according to what the customers in each segment buy. Then merchandise category managers refer constantly to characteristics of the MyLife segments to determine which customers are buying what products. By evaluating its assortment from a customer lifestyle segment point of view, rather than just a category perspective, Kroger makes merchandise buying decisions in a way that caters to its most important segments.[6] Kosher butter has high exclusivity, whereas Land O'Lakes butter has lower exclusivity, because customers will substitute other brands if they go on sale or if Land O'Lakes is out of stock. However, Land O'Lakes butter has higher penetration, because relatively fewer customers seek out kosher options. The degrees of penetration and exclusivity then influence the sales measure.

The key for Kroger is to merge both traditional sales measures with novel customer engagement measures to create actionable strategies.[7] Kroger incorporates what it learns about

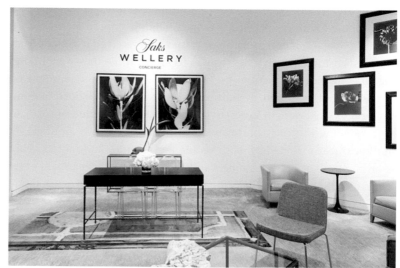

Image 3.1
The Wellery temporarily offered concierge gym services inside of Saks Fifth Avenue's flagship store in New York City

Source: Saks

different customer segments into actionable merchandise assortment plans that correspond to the meaning those customers associate with various products.

CVS goes beyond just understanding its customers, by working with suppliers that can guarantee they will provide the assortment needed to meet customer expectations. Noting that customers confronting out-of-stock situations simply did not make a purchase in approximately 75 percent of cases, CVS added collaborative planning, forecasting, and replenishment (CPFR) tools to its operations. As a result, it increased stock levels and sales, even as it reduced inventory levels. That is, by planning in advance and working closely with suppliers, CVS was able to determine what each of its products really meant to consumers – and define which ones it needed to carry or not – to improve its operations.[8]

 **A Little Bit About ...**

CVS[9]

The first CVS Store was founded in 1963 in Lowell, Massachusetts. The initials CVS stand for 'Consumer Value Stores.' Today, CVS Health has emerged as a revolutionary pharmacy company, reconceptualizing the very role that pharmacies can play in health care. It is the largest (and still growing) pharmacy provider in the United States, with net revenues of more than $170 billion in 2016, more than 9,700 retail locations under the CVS/Pharmacy and Longs Drugs Stores banners, over 1,000 walk-in CVS/Minute clinics, and 240,000 employees. CVS Health is an international company. CVS/Pharmacy maintains an extremely large reward program, ExtraCare®, with over 60 million active member households.

In 2007 CVS and Caremark Rx, Inc., merged and created CVS/Caremark. The customers this division serves range from government groups, firms, health insurance companies, and managed care plans. The many services offered include pharmacy services, discounted drug purchase arrangements, and disease management services.

CVS/Caremark has set itself apart as an innovator by using its impressive information systems to provide a variety of services, from drug interaction screenings to providing patients with generic information, and much more. Furthermore, clients can take advantage of the services offered online at caremark.com.

Adding On: How Can Retailers Build Assortments that Provide Incremental Sales?

Part of value entails getting customers to shop more often with the focal retailer and spend more on each trip. Therefore, merchandise decisions must address incremental sales – that is, those sales that would not have taken place without the presence of certain products on the store's shelves. At CVS for example, a test project inserted various types and modes of pain relief supplies together in a single display. By adding options beyond traditional pills designed to relieve pain, the drugstore display evoked powerful consumer responses; CVS quickly expanded this experiment to most of its stores.[10] (We discuss the power of display designs to spark excitement later in this chapter.)

Part of what makes CVS so innovative on this front is the speed with which it experiments and implements additions in its 'what' decision making, in an effort to maintain excitement. Innovative retailers create excitement and value when they actively introduce merchandise that features innovations or offer value-added services that encourage customers to participate in categories in which they have not previously been shopping.

Taking Away: How Do Retailers Decide Which Items to Delete from the Assortment?

There may have been a time when the goal of increasing sales could be accomplished by adding new merchandise categories, but today, the game has changed dramatically. In an effort to maintain high levels of productivity in limited space, adding SKUs with greater potential returns now necessitates the deletion of less productive ones. By reviewing customer segments, and making delisting decisions on the basis of customer preferences instead of just category characteristics, innovative merchandise category managers can determine which candidates will have the least negative overall impact. That is, innovative retailers understand

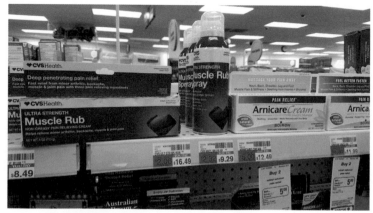

Image 3.2
The pain relief shelves at a CVS store represent an innovative approach to organizing merchandise

Source: Jerry Coyne, https://whyevolutionistrue.wordpress.com

that they need to fine-tune the amount of merchandise they carry, relative to customer expectations.[11] Aldi asserts that its customers neither want nor need '50 different types of toilet paper,' so it can limit its assortment drastically while still giving shoppers what they want and value.[12]

The toothpaste aisle offers an apt example. Retail shelves host whitening, plaque fighting, sensitivity reducing, and anti-gingivitis versions, to name just a few, all in a multitude of flavors and sizes – with each and every option offered by every brand that the store carries! To carry a full assortment, retailers would have to stock more than 300 distinct types and sizes of toothpaste.[13]

But innovative retailers are taking greater care to assess the productivity of every single product they carry, balancing that with its space requirements. Supervalue has chosen to limit its toothpaste units.[14] Kroger's response is a little more complicated. The retailer reviews each SKU in terms of its profitability, the types of customer segments that purchase the item, and the other products that those same customers purchase. By analyzing the overall shopping basket that each customer segment tends to purchase, Kroger can ensure it continues to carry items purchased by its most loyal customers – even if those products might not always represent the most profitable ones for the retailer.[15]

To counteract this continued proliferation of available SKUs, retailers also are rationalizing their assortments through careful editing. In the past, they might have edited their assortments by ranking the products according to their sales and profits, such that those on the low end would be the first cut. The approach might seem reasonable, but it probably does not result in the most productive or exciting assortment.[16] Instead, as Kroger recognizes, the retained items must be those demanded most by their best customers – that is, the items

Image 3.3
Extensive toothpaste options in supermarkets can quickly become overwhelming for shoppers

Source: Bai-Bua's Dad / Shutterstock.com

that create the most value. If an item, or items provided by a certain vendor, does not attract the retailer's best customers, replacement is appropriate. The continuous process of carefully editing assortments prompts competitive market advantages and customer loyalty, because the best customers are excited to realize that the store is working hard to appeal to them. It becomes 'their store.' Thus, the availability of the favored items preferred by core customer segments is critical as retailers go about reducing their SKUs.

Retailers should also recognize that some products might seem to perform inadequately when measured on the basis of standard metrics, but they also might make the difference in whether loyal customers will frequent the store or not. They must be mindful that if they do not carry a particular product, these customers may visit a different store. Such loyalty seems unusual in low involvement categories, but toothpaste customers, for example, appear unwilling to risk different product trials, especially when the decision about which new option to try becomes daunting due to the plethora of options on shelves. This effect is supported by research that highlights the need to maintain the space devoted to the category.[17]

The most traditional method for making delisting decisions is based on common performance metrics such as sales dollars, sales units, gross margin, and inventory turnover. These metrics should not be used in isolation, however. For example, retailers often leverage an item with low margins but high sales to bring customers into the store, because once they are there, these customers also purchase other, higher margin items. Retailers taking a customer-oriented approach thus analyze their best customer groups' market baskets – that is, the set of products that customers buy together during a shopping trip.

As we mentioned previously, at Kroger, in-depth analyses of SKUs and categories rely on its MyLife segmentation scheme. At the aggregate level, it might appear as if few customers get excited about or buy a given product, when the analysis at the segment level might suggest that virtually every customer in a particular segment buys it. Because people within this lifestyle segment consistently purchase this same product, managers recognize that it probably offers them important value, in terms of helping them define their identity. If instead a product is purchased by a few customers across a wide variety of MyLife segments, its deletion could have a less negative impact. Furthermore, if a product is bought only inconsistently, by no particular lifestyle segment, viable alternatives likely exist that will appeal more consistently to customers in any lifestyle segment – because it offers them more value.

Allocating Merchandise to Stores: The 'When and Where'

At one time, every customer who entered a store was likely to be well known to the retailer, whether it was the neighborhood grocer on the corner or the dry goods merchant. These purveyors have stayed prominent in American consumers' imaginations when they think about what retailing should look like. Although the reality differs – none of the CEOs we interviewed could claim to know her or his customers personally – innovative retailers still aim to make people feel as if this ideal persists. That is, if shoppers visit a nearby store and find exactly the type and varieties of items that they were searching for, it creates the thrilling sense that the retailer knows them.

Even though maintaining local, customized assortments tends to be more challenging for modern, global retailers – demanding greater effort and devoted tactics – the benefits are more than worthwhile for those at the cutting edge. For example, recognizing that urban customers still need a corner grocer for their milk, eggs, and office supplies, CVS creates urban store assortments that include these elements, rather than forcing city dwellers to get in their cars and drive to the suburbs.[18] That is, CVS seeks to offer a 'general store' on the corner for its urban customers. With these offerings, it has enhanced sales in these stores by 8 percent and its profitability by 9 percent.[19]

With a somewhat different approach, Sweden's ICA grocery chain includes stores owned by individual entrepreneurs, who are very knowledgeable and active in their individual markets.[20] None of the stores is exactly the same. Although each new store receives guidelines from ICA, which the chain has developed through experience and over time, each store is somewhat different, reflecting the preferences of its local customers.[21]

It should be clear from these examples that decisions about merchandise allocation can take different forms. Accordingly, we divide our discussion into two main parts: when and where innovative retailers allocate their merchandise across markets, and when and where innovative retailers place their merchandise within stores.

When and Where to Send Merchandise Across Markets

Assortment localization is a tactic that allows retailers to use inventory management software to tailor their retail assortments for different geographic areas to appeal specifically to local clientele. Modern analytics and data management systems are so sophisticated that retailers can quickly and efficiently determine exactly which items sell best in which stores and in which months, then allocate their inventory accordingly. This technology focuses on getting the right quantities of appropriate products to the right locations when the customer needs it. Interestingly, such allocation decisions have greater impacts on profitability than does the decision about the exact quantity of merchandise to purchase.[22]

At Macy's, localization represents one of its most notable recent initiatives. Even the name of the initiative, 'MyMacy's,' evokes the personalized approach the chain is taking to its assortment decisions. Some of this initiative resulted from the damage Macy's suffered by ignoring customers' desires for localization. For example, when it bought the Marshall Field's chain and standardized that chain's State Street location, Chicagoans protested vigorously.

A Little Bit About ...

Macy's[23]

Macy's Inc. was established in 1858; today, it is one of the foremost retailers in the United States, earning over $25 billion in 2016 and employing 140,000 people. There are more than 800 stores across 45 states, Washington DC, Puerto Rico, and Guam, managed by Macy's Inc. under the Macy's and Bloomingdale's brands. Macy's Inc. also includes Bloomingdale's outlet stores, Bluemercury, Macy's Backstage, macys. com, and bloomingdales.com. The Macy's brand seeks a positioning as a place to find an impressive assortment of top brands with great value and the promise of 'the magic of Macy's.' It creates magic and excitement through various events, including well-known and beloved holiday traditions, such as the famous Thanksgiving Day Parade and arrival of Santa Claus, engaging window displays, tree lightings, and Fourth of July fireworks. Macy's also works to keep the magic alive all year round, with flower and fashion shows, cooking demonstrations, and celebrity appearances. The Bloomingdale's brand sets itself apart from the mainstream by being the only full-line, upscale department store in the United States to feature notable brands such as Armani, Burberry, Chanel, Christian Dior, Gucci, Jimmy Choo, Louis Vuitton, Prada, and more. There are 38 stores under this banner, as well as 173 outlet stores.

The reason for its attempt to standardize – efficiency! – has not disappeared though, so Macy's turned to technological advances that would enable it to pursue a new and valuable compromise: centralized business processes combined with localized assortment decisions. Its New York-based merchandise team makes a vast number of the decisions about the clothing sizes to order – by category and by vendor – for all stores in the country.[24] This team crunches vast data to determine how well the orders match the sizes that people actually buy. They also take into account seasonality.

With this information, district planners, who are responsible for around 10 stores each, then gather more data from salespeople and customers regarding necessary adjustments for the merchandise allocations to the various stores. Of course, the feedback goes both ways, such that the district planners report back to the size team to suggest any necessary adjustments. For example, the buyers in Columbus, Ohio, added more golf shirts, shorts, and visors to their stores, after realizing that Ohioans were wearing these to church and casual lunches, in addition to while golfing. The MyMacy's staff had a 'primary job ... to see what those customers wanted – and then get it for them.'[25]

In its sophisticated partnership with Dunnhumby, the customer insight firm, Macy's analyzes customers' behavior to support a segmentation strategy based on purchase behaviors.

By determining how to encourage certain behaviors by people living in different locales, Macy's can make assortment decisions that support its overall goals and ensure customer value.

In a similar fashion, Saks Fifth Avenue knows exactly who is likely to come through the doors of its Manhattan flagship store: she will be 46–57 years old, embrace a 'classic' style for her work clothes but want more modern looks for her weekends.[26] By stocking Chanel and Gucci, Saks ensures that this typical customer feels as though she can get exactly what she wants every time she arrives. But in Greenwich, Connecticut, just a short train ride away, Saks' primary customer is older and more likely to stay home. In Stamford, Connecticut, five miles down the road, a Saks shopper probably commutes to New York for work. With such detailed information about customers whose locales differ only slightly, Saks can ensure it gives each shopper the feeling that she (or he, in some cases) is entering a neighborhood store that provides exactly what she was looking for when she decided to begin shopping.

This home-style appeal gives the store an advantage by differentiating it from others. And the tactic certainly is not limited to high-end clothing retailers, as the trend toward smaller, neighborhood markets instead of supercenters shows. Mega-retailers such as Target and Walmart look to design carefully edited assortments in smaller stores. Target's localized sites offer up to 90 percent of the categories found in a SuperTarget, but they contain smaller assortments within each category.[27] Similarly, rather than making customers drive to a major city to find a NikeTown, Nike is opting for smaller stores, which also simplify the customer's shopping experience.[28]

Such simplified and appealing allocations, such that the store feels like a neighborhood market, offer value not just for consumers but naturally for the retailer as well. Stores with effective, efficient allocations earn more revenue per square foot. They use their space more wisely, so their inventory holding costs decline. Because the allocation is effective, customers buy virtually all the items the retailer stocks, so it does not have to worry about markdowns or out-of-season clutter.

When and Where to Place Merchandise in the Store

Both real-world evidence and research suggest the vast importance of creating a store environment that is fun, exciting, and pleasant to experience. The resulting 'revolution in sensory marketing techniques' spans 'virtually every product category' and relates to 'visual, auditory, tactile, olfactory, and gustatory aspects of the store environment.'[29] This is a fancy way of saying that by leveraging different aspects of the store – including the placement of products – innovative retailers create exciting, distinct environments that get shoppers in the mood to buy.[30]

Consider some experiments conducted recently in and with the cooperation of ICA stores. Digital signs were on for three weeks in two stores (signage on) and off for those three weeks in another two stores (control stores). After three weeks, the digital signs were on in the former control stores and off in the former three-week signage-on stores. Information on shopping time and store sales demonstrated a significant lift when the stores had the signage on.[31]

Image 3.4
Supermarkets
are increasing
their uses of
digital displays to
attract shoppers'
attention

Source: Jens
Nordfält

The Role of Digital Displays and Sensory Cues in Drawing Attention to Merchandise

In another experiment, researchers examined the role of placing a bright red triangular sign on the floor in front of a display for jams. Therefore, in the study, the experimental stores had the sign and the control stores did not use any signs. After the first time period, the stores were switched (e.g., the experimental stores became control stores and did not have the floor sign). Customer perceptions were measured using surveys, and walking patterns were assessed using ceiling cameras. The data from the cameras demonstrated that more customers walked down the aisle when the sign was on the floor, and the surveys indicated that they found the display to be more organized and purchased more displayed items.[32]

Scent and lighting in the store also create excitement, according to tests again run in ICA stores. For example, when a scent machine was placed near shampoo aisles that released a pleasant scent next to the display for a new shampoo, it elevated customers' moods, the store was viewed more positively, and they made more unplanned shampoo purchases and other products in the proximity of the scent.[33]

To understand how ambient lighting might affect product perceptions, researchers examined the role of blue light bulbs (vs. traditional light bulbs) adjacent to oral care product displays. Customers rated the oral care products more innovative and of higher value when exposed to the blue lights as opposed to the traditional lighting. They also made more unplanned purchases.[34]

Such influences tend to be particularly prominent for impulse products (e.g., candy bars). For example, in an experiment conducted by researchers in conjunction with Coop Forum convenience stores, the retailer placed candy either alone on a display or near a staple product, coffee. When the candy bars were next to the coffee, their sales increased by 10 percent, and customers reported higher purchase intentions, evidently because the exciting thought of pairing a little chocolate with their coffee was enough to prompt them to buy.[35]

As these experiments, conducted in conjunction with ICA and Coop Forum, show innovative retailers recognize that they can learn a lot from in-store experiments: they can be easily implemented at low costs, and they can help retailers determine how their 'where and when' decisions are likely to influence consumers' excitement and thus their behaviors.

Pricing and Promoting the Merchandise: The 'How'

The Value Function, as depicted in Figure 3.2, emphasizes the overarching importance of providing customers with good value. Value refers to benefits received relative to price paid.[36] Value should be signaled and operationalized using appropriate pricing cues. By assigning appropriate prices and implementing effective price promotions for appropriate merchandise, innovative retailers get customers excited about buying the offerings they provide, which ensures more profitability for the retailer. In this section, we outline several key pricing tactics, including the role of internal reference prices.[37]

For some products, especially those that they buy frequently, customers already have an appropriate price in mind. These products, such as milk or detergent in supermarkets, are easy for customers to compare, because they buy them all the time. To ensure value, an innovative retailer must keep these frequently purchased SKUs in stock at all times, as well as apply frequent promotions to offer lower prices than competitors. That is, the retailer should benchmark the price of these SKUs against customers' internal reference price – and then beat that price. Accordingly, customers perceive great value, and these SKUs achieve a high inventory turnover.

Figure 3.2
The value scale

With this perception based on the benchmarked price of SKUs, customers tend to make purchase decisions that reflect their desire for the best price for these commonly purchased items. Thus, Staples prices its ink and paper products – its most frequently purchased SKUs – to give customers greater value. Of course, once customers arrive at the store, attracted by Staples' assortment and appealing price points, the retailer can also tempt them with products not easily found at other retailers or less frequently purchased items. In these cases, the customer is not likely to have a comparison price in mind, so Staples might be able to earn a higher margin on those items.

Pricing

Pricing requires a difficult balancing act. For those products for which customers are less price sensitive, retailers must be careful to take sufficient margins without alienating customers by charging too much. Thus, to support benchmarked pricing, retailers often undertake elasticity testing across multiple stores in different regions. For example, Staples might test different prices of a new product being introduced in the market by charging different prices in various stores (e.g., $17.99, $19.99, and $21.99). It then combines these data with information that supports its allocation decisions (e.g., different size distributions, weather patterns) to determine the best price for the exact number of products allocated to each store in each region across the nation.

As the name clearly reveals, value-based pricing aims directly at balancing our scale. Although value-based pricing does not always mean charging the lowest prices possible, customers often shop where they find the lowest price, especially if they get excited by the prospect of scoring a deal. The shoe retailer DSW averages 30 percent off department store prices, unless it is pricing high-end labels such as UGGs or Coach, for which its prices are only 10 percent lower. DSW works hard to ensure it offers the most relevant brands, and it is willing to slash prices by 50 percent to ensure they move quickly. That is, DSW's value-based pricing methods span the different meanings of value, it can be a highly discounted price, or it can mean a better-than-usual price on high demand shoes that are normally not discounted.[38]

 **A Little Bit About …**

DSW[39]

DSW Inc. is an Ohio-based, omnichannel shoe retailer whose first store opened in 1991. It comprises both the DSW Designer Shoe Warehouse, with more than 500 stores in the United States, and dsw.com. The ultimate goal of this company is to provide everyday value for top brands. In particular, to enhance the value it offers, DSW has incorporated a wide range of handbags and accessories into its assortment of 23,000 shoes. It also allows customers to use the in-store system, shoephoria, to navigate through its expansive collections. Furthermore, DSW customers can earn points and redeem them for rewards through DSW Rewards.

To accomplish these value-related goals, DSW is guided by several core values for the company: passion, accountability, collaboration, and humility. As a place for shoe lovers, DSW wants shopping to be a positive emotional experience, where every customer experiences 'the thrill of finding the perfect shoe.' In addition, DSW Inc. partners with other retailers through the Affiliated Business Group (ABG) to help support a total of 290 shoe departments by supplying merchandise and advising them about in-store experiences.

We find that most retailers price their store brands by benchmarking against a national brand equivalent. However, innovative retailers are starting to integrate this tactic with value-based pricing of their private labels (for more on this topic, see Chapter 4). For example, Staples finds that products such as envelopes and adhesive tape already provide low prices and good value to customers, so its private-label version might cost only 10 percent less than the national brand offering. In other categories, such as #2 pencils, the national brands appear highly overpriced, so Staples offers a value-based discount of 40 percent on its private-label pencils.[40] If Staples is the only or the major player in any category, it can determine a price on its own that earns it the highest margins and the greatest velocity, leading to the most value.

Promotions

Effective promotions are those that encourage purchases for certain products in certain categories at certain times and in specific stores. They also strategically increase value for both customers and retailers through these exciting offers. For example, Staples often offers products on sale for a penny. Clearly Staples cannot make money on this sale, but it drives traffic into the store and, ideally, increases the profitability of the entire store by providing incremental profit margins that would not exist without the promotion.[41]

One common promotional vehicle is weekly flyers and circulars, which communicate about and promote products, both national brands and private labels (see Chapter 4). In the past, retailers' flyers and circulars applied conventional thinking – target only price-sensitive customers. The items were chosen in a more vendor-oriented manner, on the basis of which vendor provided the best deal, rather than the value for customers. For example, each category manager would negotiate with its vendors for 'deals' to pass on to customers and promote in the circulars. The retailer allocated a certain number of 'blocks' in each circular to each department, according to its importance in the store overall.

As a result of this approach, each category manager tended to seek out and negotiate for the best deals to promote, so the circular summarized the best deals in each category. Based on a vendor-oriented perspective, the chosen items may have only been salient to customers by chance, and most were lower priced products. In addition, vendors could purchase positions in the circulars, which meant the retailer lost control over its own promotions, and the items were even less important to customers. As a result, circulars appealed almost exclusively to price-sensitive customers, rather than to the best, most loyal ones.

Today however, circulars are more customer-oriented; they promote products that are specifically chosen to get customers' attention because they are valuable, relevant, and exciting to them. How are they chosen? First, the products that appear in a circular should be frequently bought and sufficiently discounted that a promotion on them brings customers into the store. The promotion aims to increase the store's overall profitability, not the margins on an individual product.

Second, promoted products should encourage the purchase of other products. Therefore, even if the profit margin on the promoted product is low, the store still earns sufficient margins on the other products the customer buys (recall our discussion of shopping basket analyses from earlier in this chapter). For example, low prices on computers should increase the sales of add-on software, printers, and cables. If the circular only prompts the purchase of a computer (which already has very low profit margins), it fails to create value for the retailer. In contrast, if customers buy 12 other items, then promoting the computer for half price would have been a great idea. Even when customers cherry pick – that is, only purchase the specific item on promotion during a particular shopping trip – the promotion may succeed in terms of creating an image of value, and the retailer is likely to find the promotion profitable.[42] A customer who is thrilled with the low price on a computer is more likely to perceive value from Staples' assortment, pricing, and promotions and therefore come back again when copy paper runs low or the kids need back-to-school supplies.

Kroger also has a rigorous selection process for its circulars. The weekly circular is the same for everyone, but using customer data and insights from its partner Dunnhumby, Kroger allocates a carefully selected set of promotions to its circulars that feature products that appeal to each of its customer segments. The circular thus might promote Bounty paper towels – not because Bounty appeals to everyone, but because the promotion on Bounty paper towels attracts an upscale segment. In the same circular, the promotion on Suave hair care products will appeal to more price-sensitive customers. In contrast to conventional thought, circulars are not just for the price sensitive, nor are there quotas for each merchandise category. One block might offer a meat promotion, while dairy may not be represented at all in a given week. Kroger also uses its market basket data to assure that items chosen for its circular will generate complementary sales. So for instance, it might feature deli meats, which encourage customers to expand their shopping basket by adding bread, mustard, lettuce, tomatoes, and cheese.

Promotions offer a way to appeal to customers; as the Kroger analysis shows, they can even reflect a form of segmentation. To allocate promotions even more precisely, some innovative retailers rely on 'one-to-one targeting,' which means offering each customer a unique deal that represents the best value for that individual. Thus, at Kroger, the weekly circular is based on customer segmentation models, but the targeted promotions are specific to each customer as an individual shopper. These promotions not only reward customers but also increase loyalty and the customer's commitment to the store – with Kroger's help. By offering targeted promotions based on loyalty card data, the retailer encourages customers to consider new categories, make more visits to the store, buy more private-label products, or spend more on their grocery visits – or all of the above.

For example, using an analysis of the depth and breadth of each loyalty card holder's shopping transactions in each category, Kroger can decide whether to promote bread to a customer who has never bought bread in the store before. This lack of purchase history could imply two things: the customer has found a better price for bread at another retailer and is buying all her bread there, instead of at Kroger; or, the customer avoids bread altogether, perhaps because of a low-carbohydrate diet or an allergy to gluten.

To determine which reason holds, and thus whether a bread promotion is appropriate, Kroger first analyzes customer data at the customer segment level, and then disaggregates the data to the single-customer level. Customer Z does not buy bread. The segment to which Customer Z belongs also does not tend to buy bread, but during previous promotions, sales of bread increased among this segment. This analysis suggests Kroger should offer the promotion on bread to Customer Z.

However, once it disaggregates the data, the retailer realizes that Customer Z also purchased gluten-free cake mix, which implies that the 'shopping basket gap' for bread has nothing to do with pricing. Instead, Kroger should target Customer Z with promotions for other gluten-free products, like pasta and crackers. In turn, Kroger may be able to recognize a problem with its assortment allocation. Are there many other gluten-free customers in this store? If so, Kroger should increase its allocation of appealing offerings for these particular customers.

CVS similarly allocates its promotional resources to targeted customers, using the data it collects through its ExtraCare program.[43] In addition to giving all loyalty card holders 2 percent back on their purchases, in the form of ExtraBucks, CVS determines coupon distributions according to customers' spending in the previous quarter. The short-term promotions are only applicable on the next shopping trip, so customers are likely to return.[44] As an illustration of two possible behavioral segments, its extensive customer data enable CVS to determine whether each customer considers the retailer a 'corner store,' convenient for picking up milk and diapers, or a pharmacy, which the customer visits only once a month or so to pick up prescriptions and maybe a pack of gum. Depending on the frequency of visits and basket size in terms of the dollar amount of purchases, CVS uses specific promotions designed to increase overall margins from each customer.

A Little Bit About ...

CVS' myWeeklyAd[45]

CVS Health promotes the ExtraCare® loyalty program as a way to personalize the shopping experience, with targeted coupons and offers provided through its myWeeklyAd. MyWeeklyAd was launched in 2013 through the ExtraCare® program as personalized digital circulars, which CVS e-mails to customers to feature categories, offers, and items that are likely to be of interest to each loyalty cardholder. In turn, CVS is working hard to develop more strategic personalization efforts with these ExtraCare customers. That is, using data gathered from CVS ExtraCare members' previous purchases, CVS targets users of the myWeeklyAd service, who also can build digital shopping lists tailored to the store that they most often frequent. The list will even tell them in what aisle they can find certain products. The service also gives customers customized coupons and offers. CVS, like many retailers, has long relied heavily on the distribution of circulars to drive traffic and increase sales. Today's technologies allow it to reach more customers at a less expensive rate, as well as make shopping easier for customers. CVS believes that the myWeeklyAd service will provide customers with increased convenience and create a more personalized shopping experience.

For example, for a customer that comes in twice a month, CVS offers her a $5 coupon that expires next week. If another customer typically spends $20, CVS requires that he spend $25 to make the $5 coupon applicable. Eventually, these customers become accustomed to visiting more often and spending more in the store – perhaps without even realizing why. Finally, to measure the effectiveness of its promotions, CVS assesses the incremental lift in the sales and profit margin of a customer over time. The benefits of its ExtraCare program have been notable: members buy an average of 4.4 items on each shopping trip, whereas non-members buy only 2.4 items on each visit.[46]

Conclusion

Value is a central motif for innovative retailing. To get customers excited about what the retailer is offering, the retailer must first excite them by offering great value. To achieve this great value, the retailer also needs to balance out three elements:

- What merchandise to carry
- When and where to allocate it, across markets and within stores

- How to price and promote it

Finding balance might not immediately seem like the most exciting prospect. But if we imagine retailers teetering on the edge, constantly seeking to keep the scale level, we get a better sense of how and why excitement is so critical to innovative retailing.

One of the methods we have briefly addressed in this chapter comes up with great regularity in conversations with innovative retailing entrepreneurs. Retailers that offer private-label brands, available only in their own stores, create substantial distinction along all three excitement elements: the 'what' is a unique brand; the 'when and where' are only in the retailer's own store outlets, and the 'how' is a price point that sets the offering apart from traditional competitive brands. Because of the substantial impact of store brands for innovative retailers, we assign this excitement factor its own chapter, as follows.

TAKEAWAYS

- Excitement demands value. By offering great value, innovative retailers also keep customers excited.
- Value, and thus excitement, result from how the retailer organizes its offerings, including what it carries, where it makes those offerings available, and how it prices them.
- Finding the right mix and approach represents a constant balancing act, teetering right on the edge at which excitement can be sparked.

NOTES

1 Interview with Michael MacDonald, former CEO of DSW.
2 S.J. Hoch, Eric T. Bradlow, and Brian Wansink (1999) 'The Variety of an Assortment,' *Marketing Science* 18(4), pp. 527–546.
3 Matthew Stern (2017) 'Can Kroger Make a Name for Itself in Fashion?' *Retail Wire*, 6 November.
4 Tom Ryan (2016) 'Can Fitness Classes Wake Up Retail Store Traffic?' *Retail Wire*, 28 June.
5 Interview with Gregg Mowins, Former CEO, Ahlens.
6 Interview with Linda Severin, former Vice President of Corporate Brands, Kroger.
7 Interview with Tom Gormley, former SVP Dunnhumby USA.
8 Lorna Pappas (2013) 'Retail-Supplier Collaboration: The New Operational Imperative,' *Retail Touch Points*, 5 March, available at: www.retailtouchpoints. com/retail-store-ops/2296-retailer-supplier-collaboration-new-rationale-justifies-investment (accessed 18 July 2018).

9   CVS Caremark, *Annual Report 2016*, available at: http://investors.cvshealth.com/~/media/Files/C/CVS-IR-v3/reports/annual-report-2016.pdf (accessed 9 August 2018); https://cvshealth.com/.

10   Jeffrey Woldt (2014) 'Test and Learn is Watchword for CVS Execs,' *Chain Drug Review,* 2 June, p. 16.

11   Interview with Mowins, Ahlens.

12   Zeke Turner (2017) 'How Grocery Giant Aldi Plans to Conquer America: Limit Choice,' *The Wall Street Journal*, 21 September.

13   Ellen Byron (2011) 'Whitens, Brightens and Confuses,' *The Wall Street Journal*, 23 February.

14   Ibid.

15   Interview with Don Becker, former Vice President, Kroger.

16   Sara Van der Maelen, Els Breugelmans, and Kathleen Cleeren (2017) 'The Clash of the Titans: On Retailer and Manufacturer Vulnerability in Conflict Delistings,' *Journal of Marketing*, 81(1), pp. 118–135.

17   Susan M. Broniarczyk, Wayne D. Hoyer, and Leigh McAlister (1998) 'Consumers' Perceptions of the Assortment Offered in a Grocery Category: The Impact of Item Reduction,' *Journal of Marketing Research*, 35, pp. 166–176.

18   Stephanie Clifford (2013) 'Stage-Managing Paths to the Prescription Counter,' *The New York Times*, 19 June, p. F2(L).

19   *Chain Drug Review* (2012) 'CVS Aims to Personalize Retail Experience,' 23 April, p. 1.

20   Interview with Per Strömberg, CEO, ICA Gruppen.

21   Interview with Strömberg, ICA Gruppen AB.

22   Murali Mantrala, P. Sinha, and A. Zoltners (1992) 'Impact of Resource Allocation Rules on Marketing Investment-Level Decisions and Profitability,' *Journal of Marketing Research*, 29(2), pp. 162–175.

23   See Macy's Inc., 'About Us,' available at: www.macysinc.com/about-us/ (accessed 18 July 2018); Macy's Inc., *Annual Report 2017*, available at: http://investors.macysinc.com/phoenix.zhtml?c=84477&p=irol-reportsannual (accessed 18 July 2018); Macy's Inc., *2017 Fact Book*, available at: http://investors.macysinc.com/phoenix.zhtml?c=84477&p=irol-reportsannual (accessed 18 July 2018).

24   Interview with Julie Greiner, former Chief Merchandise Planning Officer, Macy's Inc.

25   *Knowledge@Wharton* (2009) 'CEO Terry Lundgren: A Focus on Turning "My Macy's" into Your Macy's,' 11 November.

26   Vanessa O'Connell (2007) 'Park Avenue Classic or Soho Trendy?' *The Wall Street Journal*, 20 April, p. B1; also see www.saks.com.

27   Sarah Mahoney (2010) 'Target Keeps Smaller Formats in Spotlight,' *Marketing Daily*, 18 October.

28 Stephanie Clifford (2010) 'In These Lean Days, Even Stores Shrink,' *The New York Times*, 9 November (information attributed to Tim Hershey, Nike's vice president and general manager of North American retail).

29 Charles Spence, Nancy M. Puccinelli, Dhruv Grewal, and Anne L. Roggeveen (2014) 'Store Atmospherics: A Multisensory Perspective,' *Psychology & Marketing*, 31, pp. 472–488.

30 Sungtak Hong, Kanishka Misra, and Naufel J. Vilcassim (2016) 'The Perils of Category Management: The Effect of Product Assortment on Multicategory Purchase Incidence,' *Journal of Marketing*, 80(5), pp. 34–52.

31 Jens Nordfält, Dhruv Grewal, Anne L. Roggeveen and Krista Hill (2014) 'Insights from In-Store Experiments,' in Dhruv Grewal, Anne L. Roggeveen, and Jens Nordfält (eds), *Review of Marketing Research: Shopper Marketing and the Role of In-Store Marketing*, Vol. 11, Emerald Books.

32 Ibid.

33 Ibid.

34 Ibid.

35 Ibid.

36 Dhruv Grewal, Kent B. Monroe, and R. Krishnan (1998) 'The Effects of Price Comparison Advertising on Buyers' Perceptions of Acquisition Value, Transaction Value and Behavioral Intentions,' *Journal of Marketing*, 62, pp. 46–60; William B. Dodds, Kent B. Monroe, and Dhruv Grewal (1991) 'Effects of Price, Brand, and Store Information on Buyers' Product Evaluations,' *Journal of Marketing Research*, 28, pp. 307–319.

37 Dhruv Grewal and Larry Compeau (2006) 'Consumer Responses to Price and Its Contextual Information Cues: A Synthesis of Past Research, a Conceptual Framework, and Avenues for Further Research,' in Naresh Malhotra (ed.), *Review of Marketing Research*, Vol. 3, Armonk, NY: M.E. Sharpe, pp. 109–131.

38 Interview with Ferree, DSW; Interview with Doug Probst, Former CFO, DSW; Interview with Harris Mustafa, Chief Supply Chain Officer and EVP, DSW.

39 See DSW Inc., 'About DSW Inc.,' available at: www.dswinc.com/about_dsw.jsp (accessed 18 July 2017); DSW Inc., *Annual Report*, 2018, available at: http://investors.dswshoe.com/sec-filings?s=127&year=&cat=1 (accessed 18 July 2018).

40 Interview with Donna Rosenberg, Former SVP Global Pricing and Promotions, Staples.

41 Ibid.

42 Debabrata Talukdar, Dinesh K. Gauri, and Dhruv Grewal (2010) 'An Empirical Analysis of Extreme Cherry Picking Behavior of Consumers in the Frequently Purchased Goods Market,' *Journal of Retailing*, 86(4), pp. 336–354.

43 Interview with Bari Harlam, former SVP Marketing, CVS Caremark Corporation.

44   Dhruv Grewal, Kusum L. Ailawadi, Dinesh Gauri, Kevin Hall, Praveen Kopalle, and Jane R. Robinson (2011) 'Innovations in Retail Pricing and Promotions,' *Journal of Retailing*, 87, pp. S43–S52.

45   Stuart Elliott (2013) 'For CVS Regulars, Ads Tailored Just for Them,' *The New York Times*, 10 October.

46   Russell Redman (2012) 'CVS Looks to Personalize Retail Experience,' *Chain Drug Review*, 23 April.

4

CREATING EXCITEMENT USING STORE BRANDS[1]

There's no denying that people love brands. Brand names resonate with cache and cool, signaling all sorts of things about the people who purchase, wear, consume, and model them. But innovative retailers have come to realize that brands can mean a lot of different things, and their various manifestations can create excitement in a lot of different ways.

For the retailers we study, one of the most notable ways is through store brands, also known as private labels.[2] A traditional approach to retailing would have looked to manufacturer brands, with their vast resources and extensive product experience, to provide products that would attract brand-loyal customers to stores. But innovative retailers have recognized the necessity of moving beyond this option. Instead, they actively and aggressively design, manufacture, package, market, and promote their own products and services, available exclusively in their specific stores. For example, some retailers collaborate with an experienced manufacturing firm, which can leverage its knowledge and skills to make products more efficiently. The resulting products are branded specifically for the retailer's chain and available nowhere else.

In this way, innovative retailers strongly distinguish themselves from their more traditional counterparts by leveraging, enhancing, and enjoying the excitement that comes with a store brand that customers seek out and love. The examples of retailers that have made names for themselves through their brands are familiar. Until Victoria's Secret opened its stores, department stores relied on underwear manufacturers to stock their lingerie departments. But since its arrival on the scene, with its range of branded product lines, spanning lingerie, sleepwear, casual wear, and perfume, buying underwear has gotten far more fun and exciting for consumers, resulting in its strong market position in this category.

The development of store brands reflects a movement away from low cost/low value generics to strong, exciting differentiators that not only enhance and expand the retail assortment but also build a brand name for the retailer itself. In outlining these developments, we acknowledge the increasing demands on innovative retailers to manage their store brands and plan their assortments. Furthermore, we propose a continuum to enable retailers to identify their positioning with regard to private labels and store brands and plan their strategy accordingly.

The Store Brand: A Growing Phenomenon

For much of the twentieth century, private labels were primarily generics: commodity products with little to distinguish them. A bag of sugar was a bag of sugar. For some consumers, the generic or unbranded option allowed them to buy a basic staple for less money than a national brand. The national brand does not provide extra value to these customers.

Image 4.1
Amazon
store brands
compete very
effectively
with other
manufacturers
in basic
product
categories

But in the modern marketing environment, the presence of large, powerful retailers, including Kroger, Amazon, Walmart, Carrefour, and Target, has made it difficult for consumers to recognize the difference between store and national brands, because these giant retailers offer a vast range of store brands that appeal to several target markets and are sold at multiple quality/price points, alongside the manufacturer-branded products. For example, Macy's has benefited from developing and offering store brands such as Alfani, bar III, the JM Collection, INC, Giani Bernini, and Style & Co.[3]

Kroger manages its own store brands as if they were separate vendors, demanding high quality standards and price competitiveness. The grocer even requires that its store brands earn 50 percent higher rankings than national brands in taste tests. In response, customers express their loyalty to the store brands, which in turn enhances their loyalty to the store. Only Kroger carries Kroger's store brands; consumers can't go to Safeway and ask for a Kroger brand. The retailer in turn can brag that over 99 percent of its loyal and premium customers consistently buy its private-label brands.[4] Yet Kroger also takes a broad perspective on its use of store brands. It rejects the simplistic choice of only developing store brands or only selling name brands. Rather, it acknowledges that it is important to find the right mix between both options, to keep customers excited about the offerings available throughout the store.[5]

Amazon and Walmart also have jumped into this space, sensing the enormous potential of store brands and the vast benefits they offer, from a complete control of the supply chain to greater margins. Amazon actively competes in numerous categories with its own store brands, including batteries, grocery items, home goods, and pet supplies, not to mention its famously private labels Alexa and Echo devices. In food categories, Amazon offers Happy Belly (for kitchen basics like coffee), Mama Bear (baby products), and Wickedly Prime (snack products). Batteries with its AmazonBasic brand make up approximately one-third of all online battery sales; its Amazon Elements baby wipes account for 16 percent of that market.[6] Furthermore, when it purchased Whole Foods, it immediately added all of the grocer's 360 product lines to its site.

When Walmart purchased Jet.com for $3.3 billion, it hoped to expand its reach and appeal to a wider set of consumers. Accordingly, its strategy for Jet is distinct, focused on upscale private label goods that hold appeal for 'metro millennial' shoppers. For example, it will bring in organic produce (as well as dozens of other high-end household items) under a new grocery private label that it will call Uniquely J. But it is still a Walmart company, which means that it prioritizes pricing decisions. To get shoppers excited about its options, Jet offered a 5 percent cashback bonus for orders placed during September and October, such that people could earn up to $50 in credit that they could apply to holiday purchases from the site. Thus, the company hopes to have it both ways: attract a new market of hip shoppers with exclusive private-label options while still staying true to its loyal cohort of price-driven customers.[7]

As these examples highlight, innovative retailers develop an arsenal of store brand options: premium brands with quality comparable to the best national brands, copycats that mimic

Image 4.2
Jet.com's new
private label,
Uniquely J,
will be high
end but
still price
conscious

existing national brands, exclusive brands developed in cooperation with a manufacturer but sold solely by the retailer, and self-referencing brands that take the same name that appears above the entrance to the store. This range is driven by a belief that 'the role of the private label is not just to offer the same quality at a lower price, but to give a choice of different qualities at different prices.'[8] Through these different approaches to private labels, retailers achieve three main objectives, as we outline in the next section.

Store Brands Create an Exciting Destination

The explosion of store brands reflects retailers' recognition of three main benefits. Store brands:

1   Enhance and expand the store's assortment, filling in gaps left by existing brands and devising exciting new options;
2   Create strong, exciting brands; and
3   Differentiate the retailer as an exciting destination.

The private-label journey undertaken by ICA Gruppen reflects these three outcomes. When ICA determined that it wanted its store brand to be its customers' first choice, it developed a three-step strategic plan.

First, it built customer confidence in its private labels by offering great products at great prices (i.e., value). In so doing, it addressed several gaps, as perceived by consumers, especially those related to its high-quality product offerings.

Second, from this foundation of confidence, it sought to affirm and establish its position by developing a 'value ladder' that customers could move up or down, as they preferred.

Image 4.3
Inside an ICA Store, showing the range of options available to shoppers

Source: Carl-Philip Ahlbom

The rungs on this ladder reflected the different store brands that ICA developed. In turn, customers could find a variety of options based on what they wanted, from a luxury product line that enabled them to enjoy sumptuous treats to value options that got people excited about the deal they were getting.

Third, once established in the private-label market, ICA aimed to set the standard in each category in which it maintained products, such that it engaged in its own innovation, market research, and new product development. The products it has developed are unique to the chain and available nowhere else. As a result of these exciting trends, ICA Gruppen has increased its private-label share to over 20 percent.[9]

This discussion and example focuses on a physical destination, but online retailers similarly are introducing more and more private-label brands, in their attempts to excite shoppers. As we noted, Jet.com maintains Uniquely J; Amazon offers several exclusive product lines (e.g., AmazonBasics, Wickedly Prime); and Brandless.com is a new entrant to the market that only sells its own 'unbranded' products. Consumers thus find ready access to unique offerings, often at lower prices and with greater convenience than they might find in conventional stores.[10]

Enhance and Expand Assortments

Retailers examine their assortments to make sure they are providing what their customers want. Based on this research, they may introduce an innovative, new, store-branded product that is not being offered by national brand vendors, or else a product that they can provide at a better value – or both. The store brand program also may be structured explicitly to appeal to different customer segments, offering different products suitable for different groups.

Staples carries a lot of shredders, produced by a lot of different manufacturers, but when the company's market researchers followed customers around their homes for a few days, they saw an opportunity that most manufacturers had missed. When people get their mail and sort through it, they tend to be standing in their kitchens. They don't go into their home offices, they don't sort it at the recycling bin, and they don't set it aside to be organized later. Instead, they wind up with a stack of junk mail that gets tossed onto the counter, where it sits, in the way, until it is time to make dinner.

To handle this issue, Staples decided to produce its own branded, small shredder that could fit on a kitchen counter, the MailMate. Although its capacity was relatively smaller than most industrial shredders, it cross-cut the junk mail to prevent any identity theft, and it could handle staples, paper clips, CDs, and promotional credit cards. Compared with the larger, name brand options, the MailMate was inexpensive. Thus, Staples filled a key gap in its assortment by producing an innovative, value-oriented product for families tired of stacks of junk mail but also worried about their security.

In this sense, the development of store brands differs markedly from that for manufacturer brands, taking advantage of the retailer's proximity to end users. For many national manufacturers, new product introductions or line extensions take place to expand their brand reach. For retailers, the goal of developing new store brand offerings is not necessarily to increase the size of their inventory or assortment but is more customer-centric. They are induced to respond to customers who say, 'I need *this*, and your store isn't carrying it.' Whatever *this* might be, a store brand gives a retailer an effective means to provide its own exclusive branded item.

A number of innovative retailers benefit from this consumer-oriented perspective. The CEO of Hemtex, a white goods retailer in Sweden, explains that the company's offerings are not designed to create new trends but rather to respond quickly to customer requests and demands.[11] Some do pioneer new-to-market introductions though. CVS works on its product portfolio constantly in an effort to create offerings that will fill customer need gaps that arise among its national brand offerings.[12]

In other cases, assortment extensions provide products that might not be innovations but that create value because of their low prices – though price savings, once the defining characteristic of store brands, are no longer the primary consideration. Many categories contain a market-leading national brand, such as Tide or ALL in the laundry detergent category. While there are opportunities for store brands in these categories, the most potential can be found in categories with no national brand domination, such as organic products in grocery stores. Whole Foods largely pioneered the branded organic food concept in grocery retailing, but competitors such as Supervalu (which owns the Shaw's and Albertsons chains) have rapidly increased the number of products offered under the organic label Wild Harvest. At the warehouse retailer BJ's, shoppers can choose between the basic Elias store brand frozen pizza and the premium organic store brand Earth's Pride.

Image 4.4
Whole Foods was the first to apply its store brand to organic products

Source: Elvert Barnes/ flickr.com

Many store brands today extend assortments by creating multiple price tiers, often referred to as low cost, value, and premium. The low cost and value tiers have long been in place; the premium option is relatively newer. For example, when Hemtex, the Scandinavian home goods retailer, recognized that its store brands had developed a weak reputation, it radically altered its product line divisions. Instead of dividing its sheets and towels by style (e.g., Tradition, Scandinavian, and Marine), it adopted three price/quality 'ladders': Hemtex Basic, Hemtex, and Hotel Selection. At the most affordable level, Basic enables the retailer to compete with its low-cost competitors. The value Hemtex collection accounts for 70 percent of the company's sales, representing its main offering; Hotel Selection represents its premium offering. Such premium options offer consumers quality that is comparable to that of national brands, sometimes (but not always) at a modest price savings.

 A Little Bit About ...

Hemtex

Hemtex was founded in 1973. It is now a leading home textile retailer, with 153 stores: 134 located in Sweden, 14 in Finland, and 5 in Estonia. The majority of the stores are owned by Hemtex, though 15 are franchises. In turn, Hemtex is wholly owned by ICA Group. The Hemtex brand is known for selling home décor in general, though with a strong focus on textiles (e.g., sheets, towels). In 2017, its net sales reached 1,078 million SEK (~US$127 million).[13]

Because Kroger's vision involves building loyalty among customers using strong store brands that are exclusive to the retailer, it pursues a similar multiple-tier store brand strategy to appeal to all customer segments with Kroger products. In the ice cream category, for instance, it offers the 'Value' brand for its price-sensitive customers, with 'adequate' packaging and quality. In the middle is the 'Banner Brand,' which is geared to the customer that wants ice cream comparable to the name brand Breyers. At the higher end is the 'Private Selection' brand, which competes with the national manufacturers Dove or Haagen-Dazs. Developing products for all these customer segments means that Kroger closes any gaps in the ability of its current assortment to meet customers' needs.

It is not necessary to develop all three tiers in every product category though. For commodities with minimal differentiation (e.g., sugar), Kroger limits the assortment to two store brands, Value and Banner – though it recently has added a specialty line of organic sugar, 'Simple Truth' (which was previously known as Private Selection Organic).[14] The flower selection in its stores consists of only the higher 'Private Selection' label. Knowing that flowers, a hedonic product, must be alive and attractive if they are to sell, Kroger assumes it can target mainly upscale or aspirational customers willing to spend money simply to make their homes more beautiful. Similarly, exclusive store-baked breads, pies, and cookies are branded 'Private Selection' and offered in the bakery department, whereas in the regular bread aisle, packaged bread carries the Banner and Value brand labels.[15]

Coordinating store brands within and across categories is difficult. At Kroger, in the past, the category managers had control of the store brands within their category. For example, the category manager for canned soup bought national brands like Campbell's and Progresso and also managed the store brands. The category manager would control the store brand's packaging, pricing, promotion, and even the brand's name. Because of this relative autonomy, Kroger had over 40 store brand names, which resulted in little synergy among the brands, and each brand had relatively low customer recognition. Through an extensive editing process, Kroger developed a simple (remember from Chapter 2 that innovative retailers keep it simple) and straightforward structure that stresses a consistent vision for each brand. Customers have come to recognize and demand these store brands, resulting in synergies across categories. So, if a customer likes Kroger's 'Private Selections' ice cream, he is also likely to be drawn to its 'Private Selections' Angus beef or artisan breads.

Using these various tactics to round out their assortment, savvy retailers have largely committed to elevating their store brands into exciting options that compete handily with the national brands on their shelves. These products are being developed and brought to market through methods similar to those national brands use.

Create Strong Brands

As we mentioned in the previous section, store brands and manufacturer brands often achieve different goals. But developments in the retail marketplace, including the increasing power of retailers, has meant that some of these goals are starting to align. In particular, the power of store brands holds great appeal for innovative retailers developing them. We have detailed some price considerations in the previous section; here we focus on the product and packaging elements, which help maintain strong, exciting brands.

For Kroger, the product choice depends on its 'right to win.' That is, customers must perceive that Kroger can create a good product in that category. Because Kroger manages its own dairies and produces its own store-branded cheese, it is more likely to enjoy success in a related category, such as ice cream. In contrast, as a grocer associated mainly with food retailing, Kroger currently lacks the right to win in a farther afield category, like cosmetics, where it has no such capability. Building a brand requires that customers recognize the brand. In the ice cream category, Kroger therefore renamed its 'Deluxe' brand as 'Kroger Deluxe.' In this area, where Kroger enjoys a strong right to win, customers pair their images of the Kroger brand name – including good value and trustworthy quality – with the new brand name. But for its cosmetics, its Banner-line brand avoids the Kroger name entirely. Instead, its cosmetics line is Mirra, without any indication of an association with Kroger.

Target also announced plans to introduce 12 new private-label lines in its stores. A couple of them already have made their mark, suggesting that the retailer has hit on an effective means to compete in modern markets by ensuring that its products are distinctive enough to draw people in to their local stores. For example, Cat & Jack is a children's wear private label that already has earned $2.2 billion in sales, just a year after its introduction. A New Day sells a modern aesthetic for women's clothing; Project 62 promises to make a mid-century design style available to Target consumers purchasing home goods. The marketing to announce these arrivals is cohesive, in that it highlights that there is 'More in Store,' rather than specifically targeting any single private-label line. Seeking to ensure that customers realize what they can find under these private labels, Target is promoting them widely; online communications also will provide 360-degree views of the clothing on offer, so that customers can get excited about the vast range of new product lines before they even visit the store.

Part of Target's confidence stems from marketing research that shows that young consumers are far less interested in specific, national, name brands. Thus, private-label options appeal

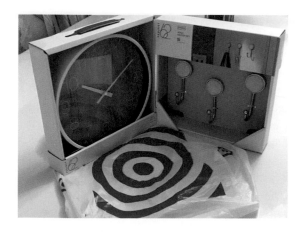

Image 4.5
Target's Project 62 line is a store brand that can draw shoppers to stores

Source: Dhruv Grewal

to them, as long as the product is good, because they have no need to acquire a national brand – unlike previous generations. In turn, its announcement of the 12 new private labels sparked approximately 900 million media impressions. In its effort to 'completely reinvent the way we are developing brands and marketing those brands,' Target thus creates strong and exciting brands through its private-label strategy.[16]

Use Store Brands as Differentiators

Outstanding offerings are always good differentiators. Therefore, if a retailer can provide outstanding, valuable products that are unique to its stores, it enjoys a remarkable and often unassailable form of differentiation. Here we refer largely to exclusive brands, which are generally developed through cooperation between national manufacturers and retailers. The simplest form emerges when a brand manufacturer uses its own brand but assigns different model numbers and designs different features for the same basic product sold by different retailers. For example, a Canon digital camera sold at Best Buy might have a different model number than a Canon digital camera with similar features available at Walmart.

A more sophisticated form occurs when a manufacturer develops an exclusive product or product category for a retailer, which then markets that product under a brand name exclusive to the retailer. At BJ's, Pampers produces the store-brand diaper, which is marketed as an ultra-absorbent option, available only at that retailer. Thus, it carries national brands, such as Pampers, Huggies, and Luvs, as well as an ultra-premium diaper that consumers can find nowhere else.

 **A Little Bit About …**

Warehouse clubs[17]

The three top players in the warehouse club market are BJ's Wholesale Club, Costco, and Sam's Club. Only members may shop at these stores, which offer a relatively limited assortment of brand name leaders and premium private-label items, across a vast range of food and general merchandise categories. They tend to carry 4,000–7,000 stockkeeping units (SKUs), unlike supermarkets and supercenters that typically carry around 48,000 or 145,000 SKUs, respectively. They offer competitive prices, achieved by cutting their handling costs when they buy large quantities of merchandise directly from the manufacturer and store all the products on the sales floor.

As the Millennial generation starts families of their own, they are turning more to such club stores for their everyday needs. Older Millennials, between 30 and 36 years of age, with children, shop at club stores about 6 percent more often than the general US population. However, these stores also face strong competition from e-commerce companies such as Amazon that actively target this market too. In response, the warehouse clubs are targeting this appealing segment in four main ways: location, merchandising, social media, and mobile apps.

Traditionally, warehouse clubs have located in suburban areas, reflecting the challenges of finding large enough retail locations in dense urban areas. However, BJ's Wholesale Club and Costco are making it easier for city-dwelling Millennials to reach them by locating them in urban areas. Sam's Club and Costco are also revamping their merchandise section by offering more organic products. In a recent year, Costco was ranked at the top of the organic retail market, above even Whole Foods. Furthermore, offering free samples of new food products is a big draw for younger customers that enhances the shopping experience, beyond price savings. Sam's Club and Costco are leading the way in using social media to excite customers, offering discounts and free merchandise vouchers through popular sites such as Groupon and Living Social. Sam's Club's marketing in particular targets young families with ads for baby supplies and discounted or free memberships. All three stores offer online ordering and in-store pickup, though the number of SKUs offered online tends to be low and typically does not include grocery items. However, Sam's Club and Costco have also introduced mobile apps that allow customers to build shopping lists, look for specials, and make their purchases. In addition, Sam's Club's app goes above and beyond, to tackle one of the biggest issues facing warehouse clubs: long checkout lines. Sam's Club's Scan & Go app allows shoppers to use their phones to scan their shopping items and pay for them with their phone, so they can skip the line all together. With these innovations, warehouse clubs hope to grow their young customer segment.

At an even higher level of differentiation are exclusive brands with famous manufacturers or designers. For instance, the cosmetics powerhouse Estée Lauder sells four brands of cosmetics and skin care products exclusively at Kohl's: American Beauty, Flirt, Grassroots, and Good Skin. Their pricing falls between the level of mass-market brands such as Cover Girl or Maybelline, which are sold mainly in drugstores, discount stores, and supermarkets, and Lauder's higher-end brands sold primarily in department stores such as Macy's and Dillard's.

HSN effectively applies exclusive branding with manufacturers or designers, with about 70–75 percent of the products it sells exclusive to its own channels.[18] Rather than creating entirely new private-label products, it partners with well-known names, such as its jewelry lines with R.J. Graziano or Tori Spelling or Beauty from Jennifer Stallone.[19] The connections with celebrities help it develop and promote the signature lines. Some of these designers,

Image 4.6
HSN websites allow shoppers to move seamlessly across channels
Source: Dhruv Grewal

such as R.J. Graziano, sell separate lines in other outlets. Others, including Paula Abdul, are totally exclusive to HSN. In differentiating itself, whether in terms of an individual line of products or the entire collection associated with a designer, HSN promises customers that they can find items that are available nowhere else. That is, it creates a strategic competitive advantage by offering great products at great prices, many of which are available for sale only (or at least first) at HSN.[20]

The highest level of differentiation occurs when a retailer develops a store brand with its own unique identity. At Macy's for example, customers often do not realize that the brands they purchase are its store brands. Its American Rag brand enjoys significant market share in the young men's category, without ever communicating to this brand-conscious customer segment that it is actually a Macy's brand. In this case, it becomes difficult to distinguish Macy's brands, such as American Rag and INC, from national brands such as Levi's – except for the fact that consumers can find American Rag and INC only in Macy's stores. The availability of these brands is widely acknowledged as an important part of what brings customers to the stores.[21] It also provides Macy's with unique offerings, which the retailer takes responsibility to design, source, and sell. With this greater vertical integration, its store brands help build Macy's overall brand as well.[22]

The Store as a Brand Manager

Creating a brand does not guarantee success. Instead, the growth of store brands requires that retailers adopt new roles as brand managers and build their core competencies accordingly. Many of them maintain private-label teams to ensure that their store brand offerings meet the same high standards applied by their vendors for designing and manufacturing their own brands. However, in a key point of distinction, these brand managers enjoy an insider perspective on their own retail strategy.

Insider status does not guarantee sales; retailers still have to deliver daily on their foundational commitments.[23] No rules dictate how much of the assortment will be devoted to private-label offerings. However, the store brand team is dedicated to working with the buyers, according to the firm's overall strategy, to collaborate and make sure the offerings have the best chance of success. Hemtex collaborates with 'external designers to broaden our styles,' though around 80 percent of its designs come from internal designers. Noting that it would not be efficient to manufacture everything it sells, the company collaborates with certain suppliers (e.g., Singer sewing machines, lighting from By Rydens, accessories from Design House Stockholm) to ensure appropriate designs and supplies.[24]

Many retailers have moved away from analyzing a store brand at the item level toward assessing products on the basis of how they fit into the store's overall brand vision. As we described previously, this shift at Kroger necessitated a structural change. Rather than manage store brands on a category-by-category basis, it takes a broader view, across many different categories. In a conventional structure, the canned soup category manager would buy from national vendors, such as Campbell's and Progresso, then perhaps decide that a store brand should be added. This approach resulted in very different, often disparate visions of what the store brand represented on the shelf, in a variety of different categories. In soup, the store brand had one image; in flowers, it was another; and in sugar, yet another store brand image predominated. Furthermore, the category determined the product packaging and even the store brand name that each product would carry, such that Kroger was left with a confusing mass of more than 40 store brand names!

The new structure instead establishes a consistent brand vision, resulting in all aspects working in harmony: consistent packaging, consistent quality standards, consistent pricing strategies, and consistent promotional strategies. Customers can easily recognize Kroger's

Image 4.7
The image of store-brand soup should be consistent with the image of other product categories

Source: AsiaTravel / Shutterstock.com

store brands, enabling them to develop consistent expectations about their quality and value, as well as enhancing trust in the brand.

From Kroger's perspective, this approach also means it can grow merchandise categories more effectively. Through its Corporate Brands division, the company carefully and methodically identifies customer needs in the various merchandise categories, then works with category managers to develop a store brand with staying power. Once customers reveal a new need, Kroger develops a product that fulfills it. Thus, its store brands achieve the goals we noted in the previous section: expand the assortment, create a strong brand, and differentiate the retailer. By carefully managing store brands to achieve these outcomes, Kroger ensures that each new store-branded item offers greater value to the targeted customers.

In this sense, innovations in store brands do not just leverage the product and the brand within the category but also strengthen the bond with specific target customers. As does any brand manager, those who manage store brands can determine customers' needs in various ways, including anticipating larger trends in the market, such as health or organic trends. Thus, Kroger might introduce sorbet under its Banner brand, to appeal to customers watching their calorie intake. To extend this line even further, it could add green tea or pomegranate to its sorbets under the Private Selection brand.

Is it Exciting, or is it a Little Scary? Making the Store the Brand

If a national brand does not sell, a retailer can always find a scapegoat: the manufacturer! But when one's own brand is struggling, the blame can only point in one direction: internally. Assortment planning thus becomes far more complex and challenging when dealing with store brands. And all the responsibility rests with the retailer.

National brands often take charge of specific elements of assortment planning, including markdown schedules, the value of promotional allowances, and the guaranteed margins. When their projections prove inaccurate, they must also deal with the error. For example, many manufacturers grant their most important retail customers allowances for items that do not sell or buy back unsold merchandise at the end of the season.

Retailers have no such fallback for their store brands. Because private-label products are specific to the store, they have few alternatives for getting rid of excess inventory. To complicate things further, many private labels offer lower profit margins, because the retailers sacrifice their profitability to create value through lower prices. Yet retailers still incur many of the same costs and challenges that manufacturers do, such as sourcing raw materials, design, manufacturing, and transporting finished goods to distribution centers and stores. It therefore should not be a surprise that, according to one study of retail margins, private labels actually offer lower direct product profitability than manufacturer brands.[25]

In turn, retailers who employ private branding must be even better than their manufacturing counterparts at analyzing market needs and opportunities. This increased risk necessitates the development and maintenance of core managerial skills to respond consistently, in ways that minimize this heightened risk.

For HSN, both risk and demand require careful and precise planning. This retailer considers its planners 'the minders of the store,' in that they use historical trends to develop expectations by category and by brand. The predictions also reflect HSN's unique retail style, such that they document the retailer's expectations for sales during each hour of the day. HSN always attempts to buy just enough that it meets customer demand, so by the end of the product presentation on television, it plans to have sold out completely. The moment the last item sells, the product automatically disappears from the online sales site as well.

In a specific example relating to Diane Gillman fashions, HSN knows to schedule an appearance by the designer every six to eight weeks. This timing allows customers who enjoy her designs to purchase, enjoy their new item, and build anticipation for the next round, which they know will appear in just a couple of months. These cycles are uniquely and carefully planned for the various lines HSN sells, requiring that it devotes considerable resources and effort to analyzing purchasing patterns and trends.[26]

Retailers must also mitigate the possibility of introducing new brands into already saturated markets dominated by strong national brands. Macy's has never introduced a beauty or fragrance store brand, because it already carries such a wide range of national brands that no gap exists. Given the control of the category by a limited number of strong manufacturers, there is clearly no need to expand its assortment here. This level of analysis enables it to avoid the risk of jumping into an already saturated category.

As Amazon has sought to expand its private-label clothing offerings, it has uncovered both opportunities and barriers. For utilitarian, basic products (think underwear and socks), its private-label brand has proved extremely popular because Amazon makes it easy and straightforward to order replacements of such items, along with a new bottle of shampoo. It also is seeing some success in fast fashion offerings, because it can get the exciting new fashions to shoppers quickly. But in other sectors, such as exclusive fashion items or even high quality jeans, it struggles more. As we have noted previously, when consumers know precisely what they want, they often start with Amazon. When they instead are in 'discovery mode,' seeking inspiration and new ideas, the overwhelming amount of options available through Amazon may move consumers past excitement and into an uncomfortable hyper-drive.[27]

Careful analyses can spotlight other opportunities when the only vendors that offer a particular product are too small to handle the level of national production that the retailer requires. Such scenarios have been common. For example, small farmers might be thrilled at the idea of serving up their organic produce or milk to customers nationwide through Kroger's distribution network of stores. But few of them would be able to provide sufficient quantity or guaranteed quality to meet the demand by a nationwide retailer. Therefore, Kroger sees relatively less risk in developing its own dairies that eventually might enable it to provide organic milk products to all its stores.

Assortment planning for private labels is inherently challenging. Retailers might enjoy close contacts with customers, but they must constantly search for more insight into customers' shopping habits and preferences by closely analyzing their purchase histories. In this sense, they constantly take the pulse of their customers.[28]

Conclusion: The Store–National Brand Continuum

We suggest a continuum for retailers, to indicate the percentage of merchandise accounted for by store as opposed to national brands. Different retailers carry different levels of each type, such that DSW carries mostly national brands, whereas Zara emphasizes store brands. Both Zara and DSW enjoy success but fall on opposite ends of this continuum. Retailers should carefully analyze and identify specific opportunities to add store brands, guided by clear evidence that those offerings will add value for customers. Store brands are now contributing almost 18 percent of the sales in all US outlets and more than 30 percent in Europe.[29] Even for a single retailer, the appropriate level of store brands can vary significantly across different categories; at Macy's, this level ranges from 10 percent in some areas to 65 percent in others. The choice ultimately must be driven by what consumers want and what provides them value. But the vast growth of sales of private labels across the board – including figures such as $2 billion in annual sales by Kroger's Simple Truth and more than $30 billion by Costco's Kirkland brand[30] – implies the need for innovative retailers to continue exploring and expanding on this exciting option.

Still, it is never easy to determine precisely what consumers want and what provides them value. Sometimes even consumers do not know exactly what they want, or when, or where. That's where education becomes necessary – as the next E in our framework describes.

TAKEAWAYS

- Store brands, due to their exclusivity and promise of great value, get shoppers excited to visit the store that sells them.
- Private labels today encompass a wide range of quality offerings, from basic to high-end options, as innovative, entrepreneurial retailers seek to appeal to various segments of consumers.
- Developing an exciting store brand strategy demands careful, in-depth analyses to determine precisely where and how to insert a private label, especially in already crowded, competitive sectors.

NOTES

1 This chapter is coauthored with Michael Levy. It draws heavily on an unpublished manuscript, written in collaboration with Michael Levy, entitled 'Store Brands? The Store Is the Brand!'

2 For an excellent discussion of store brands, see Nirmalya Kumar and Jan-Benedict E.M. Steenkamp (2007) *Private Label Strategy*, Boston: Harvard Business School Press.

3 See 'Private Brands,' available at: www.macysinc.com/macys/private-brands/default.aspx (accessed 18 July 2018); Macy's Inc. 2017 Fact Book.

4 Interview with Linda Severin, Kroger.

5 Ibid.

6 Sarah Perez (2016) 'Amazon's Private Label Brands Are Taking Over Market Share,' *Tech Crunch*, 3 November, available at: https://techcrunch.com/2016/11/03/amazons-private-label-brands-are-killing-it-says-new-report/ (accessed 18 July 2018); Tara Johnson (2017) 'Amazon's Private Label Brands: The Complete List,' cpcstrategy Blog, 5 July, available at: www.cpcstrategy.com/blog/2017/07/amazons-private-label-brands/ (accessed 18 July 2018).

7 George Anderson (2017) 'Jet.com is Stepping out of Walmart's Shadow,' *RetailWire*, 29 September, available at: www.retailwire.com/discussion/jet-com-is-stepping-out-of-walmarts-shadow/ (accessed 18 July 2018).

8 Kumar and Steenkamp, *Private Label Strategy*, p. 219.

9 Interview with Per Strömberg, CEO, ICA Gruppen.

10 Joseph Pisani (2018) 'The Next Kirkland? Online Retailers Create Their Own Brands,' *Chicago Tribune*, 29 March.

11 Presentation by Peder Larsson, CEO, Hemtex at 2014 Shopper Marketing and Pricing Conference.

12   Chris Freeman (2013) 'CVS Breaks Down New Private Label Plans,' *Private Label Buyer,* March, p. 34; *Chain Drug Review* (2014) 'Intros Continue to Enrich Private Label Offerings at CVS,' 8 December, p. 64.

13   ICA Gruppen, 'Annual Report 2017,' ICA Gruppen, 2018, available at: www.icagruppen.se (accessed 18 July 2018); Interview with Larsson, Hemtex.

14   *Store Brands* (2017) 'Kroger Strategy Plays Up Private Brands,' 24 October, available at: https://storebrands.com/kroger-strategy-plays-private-brands (accessed 18 July 2018).

15   'Our Brands,' available at: www.kroger.com/topic/our-brands (accessed 18 July 2018).

16   Adrianne Pasquarelli (2017) 'Target Kicks Off Aggressive Marketing of New Brands,' *Advertising Age*, 8 September.

17   Jeff Wells (2017) 'Costco, BJ's, Sam's Club: Why Millennials Love Clubbing,' Food Dove, 22 February, available at: www.fooddive.com/news/grocery-millennials-love-club-stores-costco-sams-club/436490/ (accessed 18 July 2018); www.bjs.com/ (accessed 18 July 2018); https://corporate.samsclub.com/our-story/ (accessed 18 July 2018); www.costco.com/ (accessed 18 July 2018).

18   *Chief Marketer* (2011) 'HSN is Everywhere She Wants to Be,' 1 February, available at: www.chiefmarketer.com/hsn-is-everywhere-she-wants-to-be/ (accessed 18 July 2018); Robin Lewis (2012) 'Q&A With Mindy Grossman, CEO HSN,' The Robin Report, 15 May, available at: http://therobinreport.com/qa-with-mindy-grossman-ceo-hsn/ (accessed 18 July 2018).

19   Interview with Brian Bradley, Former EVP, HSN.

20   Robin Lewis, 'Q&A With Mindy Grossman'.

21   Meera Mullick-Kanwar, 'The Evolution of Private Label Branding,' *Brand Channel*, available at: www.brandchannel.com/papers_review.asp?sp_id=360#author.

22   Interview with Tim Adams, Chief Private Brand Officer, Macy's.

23   Ibid.

24   Presentation by Peder Larsson, CEO, Hemtex at 2014 Shopper Marketing and Pricing Conference, SSE.

25   Kusum L. Ailawadi and Bari A. Harlam (2004) 'An Empirical Analysis of the Determinants of Retail Margins: The Role of Store Brand Share,' *Journal of Marketing*, January, p. 159.

26   *Chief Marketer*, 'HSN is Everywhere She Wants to Be.'

27   Don-Alvin Adegeest (2017) 'Amazon Struggles to Sell High Fashion,' *Fashion United,* 5 October, available at: https://fashionunited.uk/news/retail/amazon-struggles-to-sell-high-fashion/2017100526155 (accessed 20 July 2018).

28   Interview with Adams, Macy's.

29   Nielsen (2018) 'Private-label Brands are Hungry for More of the Global Food Pie,' 6 March, available at: www.nielsen.com/us/en/insights/news/2018/private-label-brands-are-hungry-for-more-of-the-global-food-pie.html (accessed 20 July 2018); Alissa Marchat (2018) 'Store Brand Sales at Mass Retail Grew Nearly 10 Percent in 2017,' The Shelby Report, 22 February, available at: www.theshelbyreport.com/2018/02/22/2017-store-brand-sales-increased/ (accessed 20 July 2018).

30   Pisani, 'The Next Kirkland?'

5

CREATING EXCITEMENT AND ENHANCING EDUCATION USING SOCIAL MEDIA

As advanced, innovative, and cutting-edge as a retail organization might be, it takes a lot of insight and effort to keep up with the innovations in social and mobile media used by young consumers, digital natives, and creative life hackers. In that sense, the goal of an innovative retailer must be to meet shoppers wherever they prefer to be, enabling these consumers to interact with the retail entity on their own terms and through their preferred channels.

Historically, with the exception of one-on-one direct sales activities, a retailer's major touchpoints were largely one-way; the creation of content for broadcast advertising, newspaper flyers, direct mail, and in-store materials was the responsibility of the retailer. The advent of new media ushered in a more contemporary paradigm though. In addition to paid media, new categories of communication have emerged, namely, owned and earned media (see Figure 5.1).[1] As the usage of the Internet has achieved widespread adoption, this new framework provides a means to incorporate new genres of touchpoints, augmenting the traditional paradigm as the exclusive dominance of company-generated media like broadcast and print advertising continues to diminish.

Traditional methods of communication used by retailers thus have been joined by new forms of electronic media. Company websites unique to each brand and controlled fully by the retailer have become ubiquitous, supplemented by additional means of electronic communication, such as company-managed Facebook pages and Twitter accounts – all representing new means to extend the brand. These *owned media* represent ways to expand the brand's presence in the digital sphere. *Paid media* instead include not just traditional media (e.g., print, radio, television) but also pay-per-click (PPP) web advertising, as well as social media promotions on Facebook, Twitter, and LinkedIn. Paying influencers to tweet or share links to a particular retailer, another form of paid media, has opened up additional ways to reinforce a retailer's brand. When effectively coordinated, paid media enables retailers to drive traffic to their owned media, thus enhancing the loyalty of and sense of connectedness shared with customers. Third-party sites that contain reviews, mentions, shares, and other forms of online word of mouth are *earned media*. Although they have no direct control over the content of such earned media, innovative retailers realize that they can drive favorable sentiment for their brands by providing interesting, high-quality content on their owned media, then being responsive to any individual comments generated on sites that support user-generated content. Such developments also have required the use of sophisticated search engine optimization (SEO) techniques to achieve first-page rankings, drive traffic to owned media, and encourage higher consumer engagement with the brand.

Such a framework can be instrumental for coordinating the many elements of a marketing communication strategy, managing the integration of individual touchpoints, and achieving synergy in their implementation. It also draws attention to the need to monitor the effects of company-produced and -controlled, paid and owned media, while highlighting the importance of responding effectively to content in earned media that is not directly under the retailer's control. An understanding of how to coordinate owned (e.g., website, blogs, social media channel), paid (e.g., pay per click, paid influencers, mobile promotions), and earned (e.g., word of mouth, reviews) media is critical to the success of retailers in the digital age.

Consequently, two-way interactions, in which consumers generate significant and credible sources of information, have overshadowed one-way communications. Not only has technology changed the ways that retailers contact consumers, but it also has opened various new means by which consumers may interact with retailers and one another (i.e., consumer to consumer). These new technologies further enrich the ability of innovative retailers to expand the number of points of contact they have with consumers and to build and more closely manage their brands.

Retailers must be astute in following these developing technologies to identify prominent trends and respond effectively. The growth of social media is one such trend, and the shifting popularity of various sites reminds retailers of just how nimble they need to be to keep up with where their customers are moving in cyberspace. Fortunately, customers' activities on electronic media sites provide new opportunities for in-depth text mining and data analysis techniques that savvy retailers can leverage for their own benefit. In a related trend, especially in the West, consumers are virtually guaranteed to have a smartphone or other

Figure 5.1
Touchpoints in
new media

mobile device that enables them to access information anywhere but that also grants retailers a prime opportunity to find out where shoppers are and how to target specific offers to them, at just the right time.

Retailers must remain flexible to effectively appeal to cutting-edge consumers, while at the same time continuing to be guided by a useful framework for responding to unfolding events. Retailers can adopt a 'listen–analyze–do' framework for action that begins with finding and determining what customers are saying, investigating what those comments really mean, and then engaging in relevant tactics to match their demands. With such an approach, innovative retailers will be poised to predict, anticipate, and react to future trends, such as the Internet of things and the increasing presence of robot retailing.

Online/Social/Mobile Media

Unequivocally, the Internet effected a radical shift in retailing; the rise of social media has had a similarly notable impact; and mobile access represents yet another radical revision of the retail landscape. So how is a retailer supposed to keep up? The answer lies in the intersection of the three types of touchpoints – the 'sweet spot,' so to speak. That is, where content in paid media is coordinated with that on social, mobile, and online channels, retailers can achieve compelling appeals and offers that draw customers into stores (whatever form they take) and enhance sales. By also monitoring conversations on earned media, they can interact with customers and address any concerns they may have, while also tracking unsolicited consumer-initiated sentiments over time to assist in their brand management activities.

Some consumers rely on websites to reach their favorite retailers. Others like to head to the stores themselves to check out the options. Still others want a mobile app that enables them to shop quickly and on the go. And the most loyal customers will use all three. Increasingly, customers demand that modern retailers offer them all of these options, consistently and constantly, so that they can pick and choose the channel they want to use at any specific time.

Nordstrom thus has proposed a bold new plan to marry its online storefront with an innovative new way to use its physical presence. The retailer hopes this effort will allow it to differentiate its brand and excite high-end consumers who value a VIP experience, along with the convenience of online shopping. Its pilot concept store in Seattle offers customers a shopping experience that combines an online interaction with an enhanced in-store shopping experience.

Nordstrom's website or mobile application will allow users to create a digital closet of items. Once the customer's selection is complete or the session is ended, an e-vite is automatically generated, suggesting a visit to the new concept store. If the user accepts the invitation, the digital closet items are placed in a dressing room before the customer arrives. The customer receives a personalized, in-store experience where she or he can view all of the items in the digital closet, as well as any add-ons the salesperson may suggest. Visits can be quick and efficient, or the customer can peruse the brand's available selection for additional items. Purchases are then made in person, saving Nordstrom the cost of packaging and shipping the items. Nordstrom also has invested in new technology to facilitate this more streamlined and unified customer experience, offering the technology to 3,000 brand partners in the hope of keeping these products affiliated with its brand and potentially attract new partners that can add new variety to the portfolio of products that Nordstrom can offer to consumers.[2]

Sephora, the specialized beauty product retailer, also has developed innovative methods for capitalizing on customers' multichannel preferences. Although it has long maintained a good reputation for its interactive website, the company remains in constant pursuit of a strategy that enables it to reach both current and potential new customers through the most channels at the most frequent times. Its mobile app, Sephora to Go, encourages customers to sign up for the loyalty program and create a Beauty Insider account, which grants them a mobile version of their loyalty card. They can check their loyalty points at any time, as well as redeem them however they wish. Simultaneously, Sephora's in-store signage encourages shoppers to sign up for the loyalty program and create a Beauty Insider account.

Furthermore, users of the Sephora to Go app can engage in any activity they would pursue in stores. The close alignment across these channels provides a seamless experience. Downloadable bar codes also are available, which can be scanned in stores. Moreover, the in-store signs encourage brick-and-mortar shoppers to take advantage of the benefits they can gain from interacting with the retailer, either online or through mobile apps. The company recognizes that, 'The majority of Sephora's clients are cross-channel shoppers,' so it wants consumers to go ahead and use their phones while in the stores. In return, Sephora has enjoyed a 150 percent increase in the amount of mobile shopping its customers undertake.[3] It integrates these efforts with its constantly evolving loyalty program, in an effort to become nearly irresistible to beauty product consumers.

 **A Little Bit About ...**

Sephora[4]

A beauty retailer founded in France in 1970, Sephora offers a wide range of products from top brands, spanning skincare, color, fragrances, hair care, and other product lines. In addition, Sephora sells products from its own private label.

Part of the LVMH Moët Hennessy multinational luxury goods conglomerate, it is not only the leading beauty retailer in France but also has grown to become a worldwide beauty powerhouse, with 2,300 stores in 33 countries worldwide. Sephora also has always been at the beauty market forefront.

Similar to traditional department store beauty counters, Sephora recognizes the value of knowledgeable salespeople, yet its expansive selling approach makes finding such staffers particularly difficult. By stocking such a wide range of products, the store format adds value for customers who want to try products from different collections, but it also demands that salespeople learn about far more products than they would have to in a traditional model, so that they can in turn teach customers what they know. To address the challenge, Sephora developed its own 'Science of Sephora' training program, covering topics such as how to identify skin types, skin physiology, the history of makeup, application techniques, and the science behind fragrance creation. Perhaps most important though, the program provides extensive training on how to interact with Sephora's diverse clientele.

It launched its US website as early as 1999, then expanded it to become the foremost beauty site in terms of sales and assortment. In 2007 Sephora launched its Beauty Insider loyalty program. With its mobile app, Sephora also allowed customers to track their earned loyalty points. The app enables customers to browse products and reviews, research special offers, and keep a digital version of their Insider card.

Moving forward, Sephora is expanding its mobile presence by introducing new features to its app such as the 'Sephora Virtual Artist,' which gives customers a step-by-step tutorial on how to apply their makeup. The app goes several steps beyond what most virtual makeup tutorials offer, in that it enables customers to upload their own pictures and virtually try different products. Yet another innovation at Sephora is its Flash service, promising customers free two-day shipping. The service is free to Insiders and available to other customers for a $10 annual fee. These technology and service initiatives help ensure that Sephora remains on the cutting edge of making beauty and technology work for its customers.

By creating pages on popular social media sites, maintaining dynamic websites, and interacting with shoppers through mobile messages, innovative retailers can ensure that their brands and identities are always top-of-mind. Without a presence in all these channels, retailers risk being left out of a consumer's consideration set, especially as he seeks social, online, or mobile reminders of what options are available. Thus, for example, when HSN wanted to remind shoppers that it had a wide variety of brands available for them to consider (e.g., Frontgate, Ballard Design, Garnet Hill, TravelSmith), it created a Pinterest board entitled, 'The More the Merrier.'[5] The board was immediately popular, garnering thousands of followers in less than a month. Whereas HSN already had many followers on

Image 5.1
Pinterest
offers a
meaningful
channel to
communicate
with
consumers

Source:
Casimiro PT /
Shutterstock.
com

Pinterest, it was less prominent on Twitter. Accordingly, it decided to expand its Twitter presence, because 'We knew that a lot of our customers weren't on Twitter. But there are plenty of people on Twitter interested in beauty products. We thought we could get those people to consider us in a new way.'[6]

Facilitating awareness takes a variety of forms, too. Innovative retailers make a lot of moves that others do not, which can require efforts to broaden consumer awareness. Thus, when CVS took the radical step of eliminating all tobacco products from its shelves, it carefully monitored both Facebook and Twitter, responding quickly, respectfully, and clearly to all consumer comments. For example, when Twitter users argued that CVS should get rid of all junk food if it really wanted to protect its customers' health, CVS responded with a tweet explaining that the company believed junk food in moderation could be acceptable, whereas no amount of tobacco use was ever safe.[7]

Furthermore, as retailers gather information to produce personalized communications, they must take care to inform customers about their methods. Transparency is key. When a consumer receives advertising that suggests the retailer knows something about her (e.g., health status, financial burdens) that she doesn't want it to know, the customer is likely to respond with great mistrust. One method to mitigate this threat is to insert icons that signal the presence of data collection tools on a website or social media link. Thus, customers know from the start that their browsing behaviors, choices, and purchases will be tracked and analyzed, so subsequent advertisements for related items should come as no surprise.

Such tactics exemplify best practices by innovative retailers. To achieve similar success in their innovative efforts, retailers today can deliberately adopt the 'listen–analyze–do' framework to ensure that their latest moves in the context of online, social, and mobile media are appropriate and compelling to customers.[8]

Listen–Analyze–Do Framework

To engage customers through social and mobile media, innovative retailers must undertake a three-stage process: *listen* to what customers have to say, *analyze* the information available through various touchpoints, and finally implement (or *do*) social media tactics to excite customers.

Listen

By systematically monitoring what consumers say on their social networks, blogs, and review sites, retailers listen to them to learn more about them. Online customer reviews – conducted through company websites, social networks, blogs, or tweets – are primary means to enact and retrieve product and service evaluations.[9] Customers appear willing to provide their opinions on just about anything, including their interests and purchases – both their own and those of their friends. Writing blogs and providing opinions via polls about such diverse topics as BOTOX treatments, Nike running shoes, or a particular play of an NFL team during the playoffs all constitute new ways that customers communicate with one another – and with retailers that are paying attention.

Macy's is widely recognized as a leader when it comes to social and mobile retailing. One of the main reasons is that it constantly listens to its customers and provides individualized responses. For example, on Twitter, every time a customer tweets about an issue or challenge using the Macy's hashtag, it receives a sympathetic response, such as 'Oh no! We're so sorry you had this problem.' In turn, the response initiates a means for the consumer to resolve the issue, whether it be contacting Macy's dedicated customer service e-mail address for social media users (socialmedia.assist@macys.com), providing a link to help the shopper order an item that was out of stock in stores through its website, or reminding customers of the phone number they can call for help.[10]

As Macy's stellar example shows, innovative retailers that aim to provide customer service through technology-enabled channels need to be constantly and immediately responsive. These customers are accustomed to immediate responses, so retailers at least must acknowledge their complaint or comment and deliver that response directly to them. The implication of this recommendation is clear: retailers that attract substantial mobile, online, and social media attention from customers must maintain well-staffed teams of customer service representatives who are trained and able to respond quickly, personally, respectfully, and appropriately to any comment received through the retailer's sites.

Customers' verbatim comments, available in exponentially expanding quantities, offer both companies and customers unprecedented access to consumer sentiments, and interpreting these product and service sentiments can reveal consumers' overall assessments (e.g., star ratings, purchase decisions). For example, with data scraping tools, retailers can scour millions of sites and use sentiment analysis to better understand their customers. They can use these insights to become more proactive in responding to customer comments, suggestions, and complaints. Numerous companies have developed social media monitoring tools and platforms, such as Salesforce.com.[11] For example, Salesforce.com might identify negative consumer sentiment and then provide services to help their client respond. Reacting to attitudes uncovered in sentiment analysis allows companies to counteract negative opinions and retain their customers.[12]

Analyze

Only 12 percent of firms report that they undertake efforts to approximate consumer sentiment from online communications using text-processing methods, mainly because of the inherent imprecision offered by many sentiment mining approaches.[13] Technology has most certainly opened up new ways to listen to consumers and take it to the next step – analyzing it. Thus, firms have more and more analytical tools to go beyond just listening.

In a social media setting, three main categories of analysis help retailers understand the data they collect.[14] First, retailers need to identify how much traffic they attract. To assess this element, retailers can turn to key measures such as hit metrics (which refer to the total number of user requests for a page), the number of visitors or visits to a site, page views (which reflects the number of times a specific visitor views a specific page), and so forth.

Second, once retailers have a sense of how many people have visited and used their social media resources, they also need to understand who they are. In particular, firms must identify what these visitors want, what they do on the site, and what excites and engages them. A prominent metric for assessing this element is the bounce rate (the percentage of visitors who reach a site and then leave nearly immediately). Another type of analysis specifies which pages represent the most frequent entry points, as well as which ones prompt the most visitor exits. With this detailed information, social media marketers can design more effective websites. Beyond entry and exit, the very path that visitors follow, as manifested in the patterns of clicks they make, is critical information, similar to the grocery aisle patterns that supermarkets track to discover how shoppers proceed through stores. Learning what pattern visitors prefer to click can enable the firm to design a more effective, more appealing navigation experience, such that those users can readily and easily find what they seek. Finally, analyses of who visitors are rely on conversion rates, which measure whether users take the actions that the marketer has sought to prompt them into performing, like buying, clicking, sharing, or donating. By combining click paths with conversion rates, social media marketers also might learn what users sought but failed to find on the site.

Third, now that they know how many and who their visitors are, retailers need to know where they're coming from – that is, where were they (virtually) before reaching the focal site? Some visitors will have searched Google or started with a visit to Amazon. Others might have received an electronic referral from an existing customer. Assuming they searched for the site, social media marketers also might investigate the keywords they used, because that information can reveal the most prominent, meaningful keywords to include on websites, to reflect how potential customers think.

Along with these metrics, marketers must establish the return on investments (ROI) in site improvements. Determining ROI for social media is challenging, however, because the revenue generated at a particular moment in time cannot be directly attributed to a particular expenditure due to the lagged effect.[15] So, instead of traditional ROI measures, innovative firms must ask additional questions: Does having more Twitter followers correlate with higher sales? Do our Facebook fans buy more than non-fans, and if so, of which products?[16]

Such analyses demand experienced marketing managers who use well-established marketing analytics software; in many cases, they also can benefit from input from experts that specialize in analytics (e.g., SAS, IBM Deloitte). At a minimum though, Google Analytics' customizable, sophisticated, free-of-charge, detailed analyses should be a primary tool for all marketers.

Do

As is true in any field, sophisticated analyses are nice, but ultimately, they are pointless if retailers do not act on what they have learned. The connections gained through social media are integral to how innovative retailers can increase their business,[17] especially considering that half of the 100 million US smartphone users make purchases through their mobile devices. Sixty-five percent of Americans own a smartphone, and these consumers are downloading billions of apps. Internationally, mobile app downloads continue to grow in every region.[18]

One action retailers can take is to use the data to develop effective personalized campaigns. Macy's has been remarkably effective at interacting with customers in ways that lead to greater sales. Macy's gains insights into its customers using predictive analytics to improve its merchandise assortment, because it analyzes shoppers' visit frequency, style preferences, and shopping motivations. In turn, it can calculate the likelihood that any individual customer will spend a specific amount in a particular product category, then present each customer with personalized offers to prompt them to make additional purchases. As a result, the retailer has enjoyed significant success; in a period of 15 years, Macy's realized a 10 percent overall increase in store sales. With targeted e-mails, its results were even better; Macy's saw a 12 percent increase in online sales in just three months.[19]

According to one recent study, personalized advertising can increase consumer responses, but only if the methods that the companies use to collect the information that underlies this personalization are evident.[20] When consumers sense that a retailer has covertly gathered information about them, without their explicit permission, they instead tend to react with skepticism, fear, or anger. At one point, Urban Outfitters designed its website to respond to each visitor using a personalized approach that reflected the customer's gender. Customers quickly realized that their personal data was collected and used and were not comfortable with it. Urban Outfitters dropped this personalization strategy.[21]

A Little Bit About ...

Urban Outfitters[22]

Urban Outfitters Inc. operates six brands: Anthropologie, Free People, BHLDH, Terrain, Vetri Family, and Urban Outfitters. The first retail location, initially called Free People, was established in 1970. The store name later changed to Urban Outfitters to reflect its target market; college-aged men and women who are educated and 'urban-minded.' It actively seeks to push the envelope, selling trinkets and clothing with risqué language and naughty imagery. Customers can shop the retailer through three main channels: in-store, online, or catalogs. The brand offers a mix of merchandise from apparel and accessories to 'items for the apartment,' all of them just a little different than what shoppers might find elsewhere. However, in 2012 Urban Outfitters took its desire for controversy a bit too far. An added feature to its website, designed to ensure that frequent customers would enjoy a personalized Urban Outfitters home page, enabled the retailer to provide different landing pages for consumers of each gender. A former marketing executive explained that the idea was to help customers pursue the apparel they were likely to shop for that day and thus improve efficiency for both customers and the retailer, so that the company could 'stop marketing dresses to men.' The new feature was met with an unpredicted backlash. Many customers were offended by the thought of being targeted solely on the basis of their gender. Urban Outfitters ultimately acknowledged the mistake, saying, 'We saw customer frustration at being targeted outweighed any benefit,' and 'If you got it wrong once, it outweighed getting it right 10 times.' That former marketing executive now works at Patagonia. Neither retailer's website includes a gender-targeting feature.

As active producers of personalized advertising, retailers need to manage their efforts strategically and carefully choose which customer-specific information to use – as well as which information to leave alone. For example, personalized advertising can leverage information that is relevant, but only if it does not make use of information in ways that cause consumers to be overly sensitive within a particular situation. Starbucks can offer marketing communications about a new Frappucino flavor to a loyal customer; in contrast, CVS should not send advertising for over-the-counter remedies for embarrassing medical conditions, even if the data suggest a particular customer is suffering from that condition.

Some retail leaders that are recognized for their successful implementation of personalized marketing techniques include Amazon, Starbucks, and Target. Amazon is perhaps best known for using predictive analytics to offer recommendations to customers; it also has a patent

Image 5.2
Starbucks
wants to alert
frappuccino
drinkers when
a new flavor is
available

Source: Basheer
Tome / flickr.com

on anticipatory package shipping. The online giant aggregates data from all prior customer activity – from clicks to shopping carts to responses to prior offers – then develops unique solicitations that its customers value highly. Starbucks has integrated the data it collects from point-of-purchase and reward programs with its mobile apps and payment systems to customize its relevant offers. Similarly, Target is using the volumes of data from its customers' store and online visits to customize special offers that are relevant at the individual level. The key is the ability to engage, personalize, and present unique offers that are easy to deliver to many individual customers at the appropriate time and place.

Future Trends

With the explosion of the Internet of things, data analytics, and computing capabilities, conventional segmentation is being replaced by newer techniques that enable firms to market unique offers to individual customers. We thus note the genesis of a new era: the *era of connected offers*. Retailers can collect data about their customers from every touchpoint – including physical stores, online, mobile, and social – then use predictive analytical methods to design offers that are unique and relevant to each one. These days, efforts occur at the individual level; the idea that traditional segmentation is sufficient has fallen quickly out of favor.[23]

Targeting customers with unique, personalized offers allows innovative retailers to employ the promise and power of segmentation even more effectively. In this sense, we are shifting from top-down, conventional segmentation to bottom-up segmentation based on revealed preferences. When Starbucks sends e-mails to customers, for example, it bases the content on data it has gathered from multiple sources, and it makes sure to recommend drinks and food options that resonate with each consumer's preferences. Successful firms use the data and related insights to develop and design offers that take into account who the customers are in terms of their demographics and past experience; where they are geographically and with regard to weather; the type of interaction, be it in-person or remotely on an electronic device; and its context, like the stage of the purchase funnel or the social setting. Accordingly, through constant tweaking of the offer, an innovative retailer can optimize its offer value.

In addition, it should be aware that it will not be the only source of every offer that its customers want. Other firms devise, innovate, and manufacture complementary products and services that increase demand for related offerings. Perhaps the best example is Apple, which may have come up with the first-order products but makes only a tiny fraction of the apps, phones and tablet cases, speakers, earbuds, and other accessories that consumers add to enhance their i-experiences. Similarly, automotive companies manufacture the cars, but they rely on software firms to develop and install cutting-edge apps, including mapping and music features, to satisfy consumers' desires for more functionality, self-expression, and enhanced pleasure. Yet the purchase, and the customer's brand loyalty, remains with the primary retailer whose name is on the foundational product.

Image 5.3
Apple product accessories are usually produced by partner companies, not by Apple itself

Source:
jessicakirshcreative /
Shutterstock.com

So in light of these transformational technologies, what key actions should innovative retailers take going forward? With regard to data capabilities, we offer four major activities:

1 **Develop big data and analytic capabilities.** The top management of innovative retailers – the ones that control the books – need to commit to and invest in big data. That means updating their storage, analytical, and computing capabilities. Kroger represents an example of a firm with strong executive buy-in to these data-centric needs. Its multi-year collaboration with Dunnhumby, which has even led to a new spin-off firm, stems from its constant commitment to understanding all the data that its customers provide it, then gathering even more.

2 **Process data, whether structured or not.** A lot of firms already have a good understanding of what to do with structured data, but it is the unstructured data (e.g., information in reviews, tweets, blog posts) that create the major challenge. And these latter types of data are only growing in volume. Although development of the tools for sentiment analysis and language coding is ongoing, innovative retailers need to participate fully by continuously discovering what's available and making use of the options that best fit their needs.

3 **Hire or develop talent to perform predictive analytics.** For managers to develop and implement new and innovative strategies, retailers must recognize that they must build an infrastructure for hiring new talent and further developing current employees – from the highest level down. Thus, retailers need to be on the lookout for talent, not just in stores or at the management level, but also among analysts, who understand how to use data and transform them into vastly appealing offers. Concomitantly, they must develop means by which these abilities can be continually strengthened in current employees as new technological and analytical innovations are introduced.

4 **Design and deliver offers in real time.** The most effective and successful offers appear on appropriate platforms, those that reach consumers where they are at the moment they want to buy. Thus, cutting-edge retailers need to determine what combination of methods they should use to communicate with customers – direct marketing, mobile advertising, e-mails, text messages, in-person promotions – to effectively motivate them to respond as desired. A well-organized system to define, coordinate, and measure the effectiveness of each offer can improve current efforts, as well as provide detailed information to direct further efforts in the future.

Once they have accomplished these actions, innovative retailers will be better able to achieve their objectives for the immediate future, prepare future goals, and devise new and innovative ways to realize them. Such advances will likely lead to an improved service experience, and accordingly, that's the focus of our next chapter.

.... TAKEAWAYS

- Innovative, entrepreneurial retailers adopt developing technologies, including social media, identify their most prominent trends, and respond effectively.
- Such technologies offer new opportunities for text and data mining and analysis, as well as new channels to reach consumers, such as through their smartphones.
- Retailers also must remain flexible to appeal to cutting-edge consumers but still follow the useful 'listen–analyze–do' framework for action. Then they are well positioned to predict, anticipate, and react to future trends, such as the Internet of things and the increasing presence of robot retailing.

.... NOTES

1 See Sean Corcoran (2009) 'Defining Earned, Owned and Paid Media,' Forrester, 16 December, available at: http://blogs.forrester.com/interactive_marketing/2009/12/defining-earned-owned-and-paid-media.html (accessed 24 December 2015).

2 James Tenser (2017) 'Can Nordstrom.com Compete on Experience Over Price?' *Retail Wire*, 24 March.

3 Lauren Johnson (2013) 'Sephora Magnifies Mobile Ambitions Via In-Store Signage, Updated App,' *Mobile Commerce Daily*, 23 August.

4 See http://www.sephora.com; Ashley Carman (2017) 'Sephora's Latest App Update Lets You Try Virtual Makeup On at Home with AR,' *The Verge*, 16 March, available at: https://www.theverge.com/2017/3/16/14946086/sephora-virtual-assistant-ios-app-update-ar-makeup (accessed 20 July 2018).

5 HSN on Pinterest, available at: www.pinterest.com/hsn/ (accessed 20 July 2018); Anna Rose Welch (2013) 'HSN Increase Brand Awareness Through Social Media Initiatives,' Integrated Solutions for Retailers, 30 December, available at: www.retailsolutionsonline.com/doc/hsn-increases-brand-awareness-through-social-media-initiatives-0001 (accessed 20 July 2018).

6 Ibid.

7 Caroline Melberg (2014) 'CVS Sets Example for Social Media Strategy,' *Social Media Today*, 6 February, available at: www.socialmediatoday.com/content/cvs-sets-example-social-media-strategy (accessed 20 July 2018).

8 See Dhruv Grewal and Michael Levy (forthcoming), *Marketing*, 7th edn, New York: Mcgraw-Hill Education.

9 Anandhi Bharadwaj, Omar A. El Sawy, Paul A. Pavlou, and N. Venkatraman (2013) 'Digital Business Strategy: Toward a Next Generation of Insights,' *MIS Quarterly*, 37(2), pp. 471–482; Lokesh Gupta (2015) 'Deciphering Customer Satisfaction Through Sentiment Analysis,' *A3logics*, 14 May.

10 Michael Barries (2014) 'Macy's Leverages Twitter to Make Shoppers Feel the Love, Generate Sales,' *Mobile Marketer*, 1 December, available at: www.mobilemarketer. com/cms/news/social-networks/19257.html (accessed 20 July 2018).

11 See 'Salesforce.com Unveils the Social Enterprise,' available at: www.salesforce. com/company/news-press/press-releases/2011/08/110831/ (accessed 8 August 2018).

12 Salesforce.com, available at: www.salesforce.com (accessed 8 August 2018).

13 McKinsey & Co. (2012) 'Turning Buzz into Gold,' available at : www.mckinsey. com/~/media/mckinsey/dotcom/client_service/BTO/PDF/Turning_buzz_into_gold (accessed 20 July 2018).

14 Laura S. Quinn and Kyle Andrei (2011) 'A Few Good Web Analytics Tools,' 19 May, available at: www.techsoup.org/support/articles-and-how-tos/few-good-web-analytics-tools (accessed 20 July 2018).

15 The lagged effect refers to the fact that it is often not possible to measure the direct impact of one specific promotional message. For example, when someone makes a purchase after reading a Twitter post, it is likely not due to that particular communication; rather, it is the cumulative result from multiple communications over time, including that post, often in different media.

16 Christina Warren (2009) 'How to Measure Social Media ROI,' 27 October, available at: http://mashable.com/2009/10/27/social-media-roi/ (accessed 20 July 2018).

17 Amy Porterfield (2012) '3 Steps to an Effective Social Media Strategy,' *Social Media Examiner*, 1 March, available at: www.socialmediaexaminer.com/3-steps-to-an-effective-social-media-strategy/ (accessed 20 July 2018).

18 See 'Number of Mobile App Downloads Worldwide,' available at: www.statista. com/statistics/266488/forecast-of-mobile-app-downloads/ (accessed 20 July 2018).

19 Mark van Rijmenam (2014) 'Macy's is Changing the Shopping Experience with Big Data Analytics,' *DataFloq*, 14 March, available at: https://datafloq.com/read/macys-changing-shopping-experience-big-data-analyt/286 (accessed 20 July 2018); Nicole Marie Melton (2014) 'Macy's Boosts Web Sales, Email Marketing with Predictive Analytics,' *FierceRetail*, 14 May, available at: www.fierceretail.com/retailit/story/macys-boosts-web-sales-email-marketing-predictive-analytics/2014-05-14; Joe Keenan (2014) 'Customer Retention: Macy's Uses Predictive Analytics to Grow Customer Spend,' *Retail Online Integration*, August, available at: www. retailonlineintegration.com/article/macys-uses-predictive-analytics-grow-customer-spend/1 (accessed 20 July 2018).

20 Elizabeth Aguirre, Dominik Mahr, Dhruv Grewal, Ko de Ruyter, and Martin Wetzels (2015) 'Unraveling the Personalization Paradox: The Effect of Information Collection and Trust-Building Strategies on Online Advertisement Effectiveness,' *Journal of Retailing*, 91(1), pp. 34–49.

21 Natasha Singer (2012) 'E-Tailer Customization: Convenient or Creepy?' *The New York Times*, 23 June, available at: www.nytimes.com/2012/06/24/technology/e-tailer-customization-whats-convenient-and-whats-just-plain-creepy.html?ref=natashasinger (accessed 20 July 2018).

22 Dave Copeland (2012) 'Online Merchants Wrestle with the "Creepy" Factor in Web Personalization,' *ReadWrite*, 28 June, available at: http://readwrite.com/2012/06/28/online-merchants-wrestle-with-the-creepy-factor-in-web-personalization (accessed 20 July 2018); Singer, 'E-Tailer Customization'.

23 The future trend section builds on and draws heavily from Dhruv Grewal and Bala Iyer (2018) 'Segmentation is Dead! Isn't It? Entering the Era of Connected Offers,' Working paper.

6

EDUCATION: THE SERVICE EDGE[1]

Text-specific Definition

What is Education?

For this book, education refers to retailers' service efforts to help educate their customers and potential customers to ensure their satisfaction, as well as to ensure efficient operations.

Customers want to engage, but they prefer to do so in a place and time that fits where they already shop. If they are going to enter into a retail relationship, customers need to feel that the retailer is a good partner, one that gives them the products and services they want, when they want them, and for the right price. It is the excitement of the overall experience that they seek, not simply a widget to purchase. But to have a great experience, they need to know how to get what they want. That is where the education element comes in. Innovative retailers make sure that they educate consumers about their offerings, the various options available, and a wealth of other relevant topics.

For a foodie making a longer trip across town to visit Whole Foods, a wine tasting is a well-appreciated form of entertainment that educates her about a wine-growing region she had never considered before. A facial provided at a Saks Fifth Avenue counter grants value to a luxury shopper, who learns how best to care for his skin. Even the knowledgeable butcher at the local grocer who can recommend easy recipes for a family dinner provides an educational, relationship-building experience for customers.

In this educational, experiential retail setting, innovative retailing comes to look remarkably like a well-produced Broadway play. The roles of the actors are shifting though. Whereas once manufacturers served as the stage directors, telling everyone else where to stand and which props to hold, today the script gets written by retailers. We find examples worldwide – Walmart, Carrefour, Metro, Home Depot – of huge retail chains dictating their lines and demanding rewrites from the rest of its supply chain.

In addition, the production sometimes seems more like a skit by an improv troupe than a scripted drama, with customers shouting suggestions from the audience. At Sephora, the French cosmetic giant, customers are free to sample products and experiment with combinations of the store's offerings. As we noted in Chapter 5, whereas department store–style counters encourage sales clerks to push specific brands and skincare solutions, Sephora takes

Image 6.1
Modern butchers provide great value, by offering personalized, educational advice about the best cuts of meat and how to cook them

Source:
Alpa Prod /
Shutterstock.com

a different route and seeks to educate consumers about the wealth of brands, styles, options, solutions, and colors available across the board. In addition, the innovative, laidback, easy atmosphere gives shoppers a reason to linger and learn more about a topic that clearly interests them – they would not have entered the store if it didn't.

The other actors in the play, the sales clerks, also are trying on some new roles in the modern version of retail. Retailers have always known that they need to train service personnel, but that training more closely resembles method acting today: store personnel need to *feel* their response, rather than just learning their lines. These attitudes benefit all the actors. Customers want to sense closeness with the sales clerks, and sales clerks feel empowered and therefore more satisfied with their jobs.

For retail and service managers then, innovative retail means coordinating the set décor to ensure that everyone learns excellence in the experience – from the top managers to the lowest person on the organizational hierarchy. Home Depot docs so by ensuring that even the CEO spends time in stores, talking with customers. It also aims to hire sales clerks with actual experience fixing and building things, because that is exactly what customers demand.

In this chapter, we consider how innovative retailers are driving the cutting edge of the service revolution by educating customers to ensure their satisfaction, as well as the retailers' own efficient (though not always inexpensive) operations. We propose the four-part grid in Table 6.1 to organize retailing service strategies according to two fundamental performance criteria: operations and (cost) orientations. Although we discuss each innovative retailer as if it functions only in one quadrant, most of the best exemplars are implementing innovative retail service strategies in all four.

On the first dimension, we distinguish current service operations versus new service operations. Most retailers' current service operations involve routine activities, performed by retail personnel: assisting customers with finding merchandise, running checkout counters, restocking shelves. But what if retailers start expanding those operations into new and innovative realms?

On the second dimension, we consider whether the retailer orients its service activities toward revenue generation or cost containment. The more forward-looking revenue generation is likely to require new operations as a means to generate incremental revenue (and profit). The backward-looking cost orientation becomes particularly popular in recessionary environments.

Table 6.1 Service edge strategies quadrant 1

	Current Operations	**New Operations**
Revenue Generation	Quadrant 1: Experience Management	Quadrant 2: Value-Added Services
Cost Containment	Quadrant 3: Store Environmental Control	Quadrant 4: Innovative Solutions

As Table 6.1 shows, we define the four key quadrants that result from these two dimensions using descriptive names: experience management, value-added services, store environmental control, and technological solutions and innovations.

Four Paths to the Edge in the Retail Experience

Experience Management (Quadrant 1)

Retailers find themselves in increasingly commoditized businesses. Large retailers, including category specialists, specialty retailers, and food retailers, have expanded their assortments to include categories that would have been unexpected a decade ago. Drug stores, for example, sell cosmetics, office supplies, convenience grocery items, gift wrap, and cards. Although their basic operations remain the same, they must educate consumers about the presence of these various product lines in their stores, as well as about the options available for each type of product.

To combat the dilution that might stem from differentiation and to increase revenues, retailers can reshape their current operations to enhance customer education and create an improved customer experience. A great customer experience means different things, depending on the customers' expectations and the retailer's business model. Kroger customers might just want an easy, convenient experience with short checkout lines, whereas Nordstrom clients anticipate a luxury, high-contact interaction with the retailer that happily may take hours of shopping fun. Whereas traditionally customers might have regarded BJ's solely as a place to stock up on vast quantities of staple products, the innovative retailer also engages in 'never-ending' education of consumers to make sure they know they can find smaller package sizes and creative options there too.[2]

We offer three examples that span diverse retail settings, though all of them focus on educating the customer, using current offerings, in an effort to improve revenues. These examples confirm that the environment in which the retailer educates consumers to ensure innovative, cutting-edge service can be widely disparate – Zappos.com, the Apple store, and HSN – but still consistently ensure appealing customer experience management.

 **A Little Bit About …**

Zappos[3]

From the moment of its founding in 1999, Zappos.com has been an innovative retailer. It was one of the first online retailers to strive to offer the best selection of shoes. In 2009 it was acquired by Amazon.com. Both companies had long emphasized the importance of customer service, so they have found great collaborative success as well, such that today, Zappos is the top online shoe retailer. Furthermore, this merger has enabled Zappos to expand its assortment and become an overall fashion retailer. Zappos maintains the powerful belief that the key to its success is its service-oriented culture. It currently has more than 1,500 employees, most of whom provide customer relations support or work in fulfillment centers, organizing, packing, and shipping orders. All its customer service representatives go through seven weeks of training. Because it recognizes that great customer service starts with the employee, it also has been ranked in the *Fortune* list of best companies to work for over six consecutive years. In keeping with its goals, Zappos demands that every new corporate employee undertake at least four weeks of dedicated customer loyalty training, during which time they answer phones in the call center, even before starting their official job. To Zappos, customer service is not just a department; it is the entire company.

Let's start online, where Zappos (now owned by Amazon.com) uses 'extreme training' to make sure its providers are offering a level of service that other retailers might consider absurd. Even if their only contact is electronic, Zappos employees do anything they can to keep customers happy. Perhaps the most unusual of its extreme techniques is its offer of $3,000 to employees who quit after their initial training. Cost cutting clearly is not the focus here: Zappos undertakes extensive interviews with all prospective employees to determine whether they fit the company culture – a practice nearly unheard of in the usually low-paying, standardized call center model – then sends those it hires through weeks of intense training to instill its customer service values in them. Nor is this educational training limited to call center workers: everyone hired at Zappos, including at the highest executive levels, must work in the call center for at least a few weeks. Even with all this investment in education for their employees, the company promises that anyone who admits they just don't fit, after completing the training, may leave with Zappos' good wishes and $3,000 more than they had before.

But if they stay, Zappos asks its service employees to virtually ignore the costs of excellent service. They will spend as long as a customer wants on the phone, even if the conversation veers far from the ordering process, to help consumers learn about what they need and want, and then how Zappos can enable them to attain it. If a customer isn't sure which size or color he or she wants, Zappos suggests ordering multiple pairs and just returning the ones he or she finds too small or not quite the right color.

Moving to our second retailer, service providers at Apple stores help take the frustration out of one of the most angst-producing issues in high-tech retailing, a malfunctioning computer. Apple customers are almost universally pleased by their experience with this retailer. Ninety percent of Apple customers report satisfaction with its customer service. In contrast, approximately 25 percent of customers express dissatisfaction with every other computer

Image 6.2
This Zappos
employee went
through extensive
training, to ensure
a good fit with the
company

Source: TopRank
Marketing / flickr.
com

Image 6.2
This Zappos employee went through extensive training, to ensure a good fit with the company

Source: TopRank Marketing / flickr.com

retailer on the market. Consider three likely reasons for this notable difference. First, Apple devices (at least thus far) are less at risk of viruses, which means that most Apple consumers need less customer service than do PC users. Second, Apple constantly works to educate its customers, whether they own a Mac, an iPad, an iPhone, or an Apple Watch. Their in-store 'one-on-one' service offer, for $99, gives new Apple customers an opportunity to reserve appointments over the course of a year with expert service representatives, to obtain personalized assistance, advice, and training. Even if they do not purchase this service, Apple users can visit the company's website and discussion boards to ask questions and review others' experiences or, if that's not sufficient, make appointments to come in to an Apple store for service. Third, Apple distinguishes itself by its advanced technological offerings. A new iPhone release and the promise of new innovations in the future create vast excitement, which increases customers' satisfaction even further – especially when the service experiences associated with those exciting devices help customers feel smart, valued, and capable.[4]

 **A Little Bit About ...**

The Apple Store[5]

One of the world's most popular brands, Apple has produced revolutionary products, such as the iPod and iPhone. In turn, these innovative products have encouraged countless numbers of people to flock to their local Apple Stores. Being known as a creator and producer of innovative products, Apple also strives to give its stores the feeling of technological innovation. It has accomplished this goal by instituting a sleek store format, bright lighting, and its revolutionary 'Genius Bar.' At the Apple Genius Bar, customers receive technical support for any and all of their Apple merchandise, and service-related questions. It has been a huge success since its launch, but that has not been enough for this innovative retailer. Now, Apple is making strides to improve its customer service experience even further with its new Concierge initiative that allows customers to describe their problem to a concierge onsite, who inputs the description of the problem into a special iPad application. That app determines the priority of the problem and assigns customers a place in line, according to its severity. However, the high volume of traffic in Apple Stores also prompted Apple to revise its support website, to encourage customers to start the process by trying to troubleshoot and fix their problems at home. Furthermore, Apple is upgrading to the 'Genius Grove' through a slow nationwide rollout, such that soon stores will house a larger Genius Grove sitting area, lined with trees, to help customers dealing with broken devices feel more relaxed.

Finally, in a completely different context, HSN is known for providing enriching experiences and engaging content through various channels (e.g., television, online, smartphones). HSN's programming enhances the customer experience by adding entertainment and educational content. Famous chefs, fashion experts, and interior designers appear to teach viewers how to cook, dress, and renovate their rooms. In the entertaining, talk-show like setting, celebrities become cheerleaders for the retailer, and customers gain insights, knowledge, and value from experts whom they admire. The celebrities and brands certainly love it: fashion designers and cosmetics companies sell greater volume through HSN's online, television, and mobile channels than through many department store channels.[6]

Consider, for example, how a customer might rely on HSN's programming to learn about and then obtain Nicki Minaj's exclusive Minajesty perfume. In an hour-long program, Minaj appears on set with an HSN host. In their wide-ranging discussion, Minaj describes her musical influences, fashion preferences, and the process she used for developing the perfume and its packaging. Interspersed with this educational content, fans get to watch clips from her concerts and images of crowds of screaming fans. Of course, the HSN host also makes sure to cover important sales details – like easy payment options, the add-ons that come with an immediate offer, and the warning that the perfume will only be available for a limited time. Together, the host and the pop star take calls from fans who have the opportunity to talk directly with Minaj and ask whatever questions they might have. Within an hour of the original broadcast, the segment gets uploaded to YouTube and HSN.com; it also features a crawl of tweets that use #NickiAtHSN. Not only does HSN.com host more than 50,000 videos at any one time, it is also one of YouTube's largest content providers and corporate users.

Image 6.3
Nikki Minaj's
Minajesty Perfume
is only available, in
limited quantities,
on HSN

Source: Eva Rinaldi /
flickr.com

This association with celebrities is a hallmark of HSN's success. Viewers can watch famous chefs such as Robert Irvine prepare tuna au poivre using his signature Personal Blender and Colorful Toss pans on television, YouTube, or HSN.com. Thus, they learn cooking techniques and a new recipe. Then, they can purchase those very kitchen items so that they can put their newfound learning into action themselves. This connection adds to the customer experience and even lowers perceptions about the risk of purchasing. As long as the celebrity maintains credibility in the area of expertise, customers get to enjoy the feeling of security and connectivity; if I buy this set of pans and follow Irvine's recipe, my tuna will be as good as his.

Not only does HSN connect with well-known celebrity brands, but it seeks out various partnerships that might enhance customers' knowledge and experience, such as those with Coca-Cola, Toyota, and Norwegian Cruise Lines. The shopping experiences people have are totally unique to this channel; they cannot obtain such a broad range of information, across so many different channels, from any other retailer. HSN also launched a totally new e-commerce portal called Boutique Univision, in collaboration with the Univision broadcast network, to enhance the experience for Spanish-speaking consumers.[7] Then it worked with a company called Mass Relevance to develop 'The 20' – a list of the 20 best products, according to fan votes submitted through social media, which gives other consumers information and recommendations they need to make more educated purchases and lower their risk. Such enhancements encourage consumers to interact more with the HSN brand and 'bring another level of excitement that we believe will resonate strongly with our shoppers who are looking for more than just a transactional experience.'[8]

Table 6.2 Service edge strategies quadrant 2

	Current Operations	**New Operations**
Revenue Generation	Quadrant 1: Experience Management	Quadrant 2: Value-Added Services
Cost Containment	Quadrant 3: Store Environmental Control	Quadrant 4: Innovative Solutions

Value-Added Services (Quadrant 2)

In this quadrant, the retailer's goal is to gain a service edge by providing expanded operations that will also increase its revenues. The expanded operations might be techno-logically based, but in practice, they span a variety of options that provide complementary services that match customer needs, meet their expectations of what they could expect from a given retailer, and provide them with more information and education in their shopping process.

Various added values are readily evident in the radical transformation of the customer experience at CVS. Once customers shopped at CVS to pick up a prescription, load up on their cold medicine and Kleenex, and perhaps pick up the latest issue of *People* magazine. Today they can do far more. Minute Clinics within CVS stores offer a less expensive, more convenient alternative to a doctor's office or emergency room visit to treat minor illnesses and learn about health conditions. For example, each November, CVS offers free blood glu-cose and diabetes screenings at many of its clinics. Customers receive immediate information about whether they might be considered pre-diabetic or diabetic, as well as counseling about what they need to do to avoid allowing the disease to advance further.[9] The Minute Clinics provide copies of the notes they create about the patients' status, which they offer to both the customer and his or her primary care physician. In particular, Minute Clinics collaborate with 32 different health care provider chains, having developed a vast electronic medical records system that helps both patients and their doctors learn about treatment options and potential prescriptions – which of course the customer can fill in the CVS store.[10]

Image 6.4
Minute Clinics in
CVS stores provide
valuable services and
education to
shoppers
Source: Carl-Philip
Ahlbom

Whereas previously, CVS pharmacists tended to be relatively underutilized, because their primary responsibility was to fill prescriptions, today the retailer has found ways to apply their knowledge by acting as prescription consultants to their customers. CVS also acquired Caremark, a pharmacy benefit manager that administers and pays prescription drug claims for employers' health plans. Now CVS and its pharmacists can better communicate with its customers about their prescription needs. Through data integration with Caremark, CVS can monitor whether customers are taking their prescriptions accurately, based on their refill rate. When they notice a slower refill than expected, pharmacists proactively contact customers to encourage them to follow their drug program. Such an effort is radical but also critical in this service realm: 61 million Americans do not take their medications as prescribed, and 30 percent of customers discontinue their prescription within a month of receiving it. CVS notes that pharmacist outreach calls and educational efforts have prompted 35 percent of non-adhering patients to restart their prescription regimen, and consultation provided at the time the prescription is initially filled has improved adherence by 15 percent. Customers thus are healthier and happier, and CVS earns the benefits of increased revenues.[11]

Non-pharmacy customers can benefit from CVS's expanded services as well. Many cosmetics customers cross-shop. They shop for 'special' products at department and specialty stores (e.g., Sephora), but they visit drug stores for the basics. CVS has seized this opportunity to educate customers about basic and upscale cosmetics through its Beauty 360 program. It has hired licensed, trained estheticians to help customers. In addition, the Beauty 360 program offers small spa services, such as mini-manicures, express facials, hand massages, and make-up applications. When customers started asking for information and help with hair care as well, CVS expanded its assortment to offer high-end brands and varieties of tools.[12]

To go along with their stylish hair and makeup, consumers also need the right clothes – an intimidating prospect for many. Rent the Runway promises designer gear for women who want to look great at a party or event to which they have been invited, but who don't have the time, money, or desire to pay for an expensive ball gown or cocktail dress that they might never wear again. Because of the unique demands and needs of these shoppers, Rent the

Runway allows customers to order the next size of the same outfit, to make sure that one of them will fit. They also can request two different dresses in the same order, for a flat handling fee.

But such efforts were not quite enough. Panicked customers who realized only too late that the bodice of a dress was too tight or that the hem trailed on a particular skirt were unhappy, even though the company already offered extensive customer service assistance by phone. Noting that customers were contacting the company not just through e-mail and phone calls but also through Snapchat, to share pictures and videos, Rent the Runway decided to try something totally different. It now encourages customers to upload pictures or videos of themselves, how they move, and what kinds of clothing they like to the corporate site.[13]

In the meantime, Rent the Runway has recruited a pool of models from among its own employees. Approximately 250 workers from the customer service department at its corporate headquarters have agree to help and offer themselves as sort of living mannequins, with varied body types that generally offer matches with customers' bodies. Thus, when the customer uploads a video, provides her body type information, and explains what she's looking for, the company solicits the assistance of a model with a similar body type. This model then tries on the chosen outfit and offers educational advice, such as how easy it is to sit in a skirt or how low the neckline falls. The customer and customer service representative then engage in further education, covering the customer's detailed questions and concerns. The plan is for service representatives to spend about 10 minutes with each customer, ensuring that the product ordered is the best option for this shopper.

Store Environmental Control (Quadrant 3)

This quadrant implies a relatively conservative approach: stick with what we know and work to reduce costs. Many retailers realize that focusing on existing operations is a key means to contain costs and improve the firm's bottom line. Of course, employees and service investments often represent some of the greatest costs to a retailer. Successful retailers thus must strategically balance the benefits of educating shoppers and enhancing their customer service against the costs of doing so. As our designation of this quadrant suggests, a key element in that balance is the careful control of the store environment.

In particular, the services that retailers provide can educate and enhance the customer experience, even if they are not flashy. Some enhancements are so subtle that customers may not even notice. For example, grocery shoppers often judge their trips on how long they have

Table 6.3 Service edge strategies quadrant 3

	Current Operations	New Operations
Revenue Generation	Quadrant 1: Experience Management	Quadrant 2: Value-Added Services
Cost Containment	Quadrant 3: Store Environmental Control	Quadrant 4: Innovative Solutions

to wait in the checkout line. Waiting in lines can be incredibly frustrating for customers, and irritated customers then stress out checkout employees, which in turn can exacerbate the problem.

Rather than revamp the entire checkout process though, the Kroger grocery chain simply noticed from its extensive market research that customers like to chit-chat. Nothing serious, mind you – 80 percent of their customers just want to talk about the weather. But the line, 'How about this weather we're having?' sounds insincere in virtually any situation, especially if the service employee asks the same thing to every customer in line. Thus, Kroger offers coaching for checkout clerks on how to bring up 'soft' topics with customers. The checkout process is the same, but the easy chats make it more pleasant for both clerks and customers and enhance the customer experience at virtually no cost to the company.

As we must keep in mind, these efforts do not mean radical changes, because the focus is still on current operations. They imply an effort to achieve the best version of current operations possible, without significantly increasing costs (or perhaps even reducing overall costs). Thus, Kroger still uses checkout lines. But by using infrared technology to measure exactly how many customers wait in these lines at different times of day and how long they wait, the company also learned when it needed to staff more and when it could cut costs by opening fewer checkout lines.

A Little Bit About …

Kroger's Analytics[14]

Shopping for groceries might be a chore, but why do people hate it *so* much? According to Kroger's analysis, it's all about the checkout lines. But Kroger is one of the world's largest grocery retailers and one that credits its success in part to its dedication to innovation. Accordingly, Kroger was the first grocery store to formalize customer research, in line with its history of pioneering strategies that provide customers with greater value. One of these research projects asks what seems like a simple question (though it's really quite complex): 'What happens when stores open checkout lanes exactly when customers need them?'

The senior director of R&D at Kroger, Brett Bonner, cites customer satisfaction as a key metric that fuels loyalty, which is especially important for low margin businesses such as groceries. And as he states, 'At the heart of loyalty is analytics.' To address the problem of long checkout lines, Kroger partnered with Visual Thinking International and Irisys to develop a system that could interact automatically with Kroger's custom reporting software. It uses infrared sensors, mounted at doors and cash registers, together with predictive analytics and data feeds gathered in real time at the sales registers, to determine actual wait times at each moment, as well as how many registers are required. Those actual wait times also get posted near the front of the store. The technology – for which the established goal is to eliminate any line with more than two customers waiting – has cut average wait times, which used to run more than 4 minutes, to less than 30 seconds, enhancing both efficiency and customer satisfaction.

Kroger's 84.51° analytics arm also uses this infrared technology and video analytics to learn what time of day customers are shopping, how large the shopping party is (e.g., a single person or a family of four), and for how long they shop. These data allow Kroger to staff its stores as efficiently as possible. But Kroger doesn't just use its analytics to optimize the in-store experience. It also uses analytics to create personalized experiences for customers. For example, it delivers more than 6 million personalized offers to customers a year through its My Magazine. As online grocery shopping becomes more popular, Kroger also uses the data it collects to provide a personalized digital shopping experience. Digital customers receive personalized recipes and product-related content. Accordingly, Kroger recently saw a 30 percent increase in new digital customers and a 30 percent increase in digital visits.

Some of its findings were pretty obvious: all checkouts should be staffed and open between 4:00 and 8:00 p.m., when people stop in on their way home from work. But Kroger also learned that it needed more staff on hand between 11:30 a.m. and 1:00 p.m. to let workers on their lunch breaks grab a few items and get through the store quickly and easily. This information in turn led the grocery retailer to relocate its to-go lunch items to the front of the store. This simple shift improved its profit-making opportunities and helped differentiate the retailer for customers – again without significantly changing its existing operations.

Efforts to monitor retail service operations, like Kroger's infrared technology, have reached the level of an advanced science. But if retailers are not careful, their attempts to exploit existing operations lead to increased pressure on retail employees. To do more with the same operations, employees face time crunches and demands for greater skill and flexibility, because they must not only complete their routine store activities but also put their best face forward to customers.

A viable option for retailers in the environmental control quadrant is to ensure employee empowerment – that is, enabling them to make the decisions about how to provide service to customers. Thus, Nordstrom keeps it simple (see Chapter 2) and establishes an overall objective for its service employees: satisfy customer needs. The way they do so is up to them. We have even had personal experience with the benefits of this approach. A Nordstrom employee once was willing to sell us a size 10 shoe for the left and a size 10½ shoe on the right, which meant we obtained the benefits of two pairs but only paid for one. The immediate impact was a loss for Nordstrom. But of course, we returned to purchase five more pairs later that day and have remained loyal Nordstrom customers since then.

Such empowerment cannot work in all settings. It is likely most effective when the service is more individualized. It also implies that managers need to provide constant coaching and training to ensure salespeople understand what vague rules such as 'Use your best judgment' actually mean. At DSW, a management-on-duty initiative seeks to help managers coach their associates better, so that those associates can help customers better.[15]

To facilitate such forms of service-oriented education, innovative retailers provide two key forms of support for their employees, consistently and coherently. First, they issue instrumental support, such that the retailer provides the basic systems and equipment that enable the employees to deliver the service properly. With user-friendly inventory systems, such as those implemented by Home Depot, store clerks know exactly how to help customers find the items they want. Registers with varied options help checkout staff move customers through the line quickly, even if they need to put back an item or weigh a bunch of arugula. Well-defined replenishment rules mean that employees always know where items will be located in the store.

Second, emotional support costs virtually nothing but can be invaluable to employees. Managers and coworkers must demonstrate concern for their subordinates' and colleagues' well-being. Such types of emotional support are a form of education too, in that they help employees learn about and understand how to work as a team and interact better with others, even difficult service customers. Similarly, any effective customer service program should include well understood rewards for excellent service. Such tactics provide emotional support but also ensure that employees recognize the great value that the retailer places on superb customer service.

Innovative Solutions (Quadrant 4)

Sometimes though, relying on current operations simply is not enough. The last quadrant in our framework thus focuses on providing innovative solutions through expanded operations. Retailers can provide access to a wider variety of services, allow educated customers to take more control over the method of service provision, and thus gain significant information and education themselves. In addition, technology-based solutions can increase efficiency in the service processes and thus reduce service costs without harming quality.

Table 6.4 Service edge strategies quadrant 4

	Current Operations	New Operations
Revenue Generation	Quadrant 1: Experience Management	Quadrant 2: Value-Added Services
Cost Containment	Quadrant 3: Store Environmental Control	Quadrant 4: Innovative Solutions

Recall those time-constrained customers of Kroger, who show up to pick up a quick lunch in the time they have available? They likely would appreciate the option to use self-checkout technology to scan their prepackaged sandwich and bag of chips. Self-checkout machines and other self-service technologies, such as electronic kiosks, are expanding throughout the retail landscape, leveraging customers' own knowledge. Home Depot is finding ways to integrate the personalized service knowledge provided by its expert employees with web-enabled devices that provide more information than any single employee could possess on her or his own.

Further examples include kiosks that allow customers to manage their gift registry, drop off film, apply for credit, or preorder a birthday cake. Even traditionally high-contact service environments can expand their operations with the assistance of this technology, such as restaurants (e.g., Chuck E. Cheese) offering touchscreen terminals to order food or salons using kiosks to educate customers about their products and services.

In all these cases, the cost benefits for the retailer are evident. Primarily, when customers leverage their own knowledge and skills to order, check out, and serve themselves, the retailer can staff fewer customer service employees. These efficiencies have notable effects on their bottom lines. In addition, by encouraging customers to preorder or reserve spaces in advance, retailers can ensure sufficient stock without holding too much inventory.

A Little Bit About …

Home Depot[16]

The Home Depot was founded in 1978 as the place to go for one-stop shopping when people were ready to make home improvements on their own. Currently, it is the largest home improvement retailer globally, with over 2,200 locations and 400,000 employees. From its beginning, the founders placed an emphasis on customer service, creating a customer bill of rights that is founded firmly in a simple philosophy: 'Whatever it takes.' This bill of rights further states that the customer has the right to the best assortment, quantities, and prices, as well as well-trained and helpful sales associates. The Home Depot strives to cultivate relationships with its customers by also offering a variety of services, such as in-home installation, how-to clinics, and kids' workshops.

Recognizing the various ways in which technology has changed the retailing environment, The Home Depot has taken measures to include technology effectively in its customer service techniques. For example, all associates receive

(Continued)

(Continued)

training on how to use its interconnected customer service program, then use web-enabled handheld devices that they carry with them throughout the stores. These devices allow associates to check inventory levels, access the Internet for how-to videos, research products, or even complete a sale in the store aisle.

Conclusion

There seems little doubt that gaining an edge in the modern retail landscape necessitates a focus on services that educate consumers while also meeting their varied needs. However, as we have attempted to show, the type of edge and the subject of that focus might vary along two dimensions.

When retailers rely on existing operations but pursue revenue-generating activities, they are adopting an experience management strategy. Because these retailers provide consistently great customer education and experiences, customers are willing to spend more. Another option is to concentrate on value-added services – those offerings that really set retailers apart from their competitors, which enables customers to learn about new options. The added value for customers results from innovative forms of service; the company attains greater revenues; employees are happy; and the innovative retailer's prospects for success improve.

When retailers work to gain a service edge by prioritizing their existing offerings and a cost-cutting orientation, we consider them examples of the store environmental control concept of service. These firms work to enhance their service without adding revolutionary new ideas or expending many resources. They seek to educate customers about what they already have in place, to make customers' service experiences the best they can be. Perhaps existing operations are not sufficient though. In this case, retailers search for new innovations, and if they are focused on cutting costs, those innovations are likely technology-based. The modern world offers continuing advances in technology solutions and innovations that improve retailers' cost efficiency without harming, or perhaps even while enhancing, customers' enjoyment of the service.

In all these cases, the roles of service employees and a service culture cannot be ignored. Whether firms expand or rely on standbys, work to spend less or earn more, they need to institute an all-encompassing culture that encourages service excellence and educates shoppers. Even when service employees play smaller roles, they ultimately are the key to ensuring an enjoyable, educational customer experience, whether in stores or across various channels – as we discuss in the next chapter. Regardless of the path taken to achieve it though, innovative retailers must recognize the importance of gaining a service edge.

- Innovative retailers at the forefront of the service revolution educate customers to achieve benefits related to customer satisfaction and efficient operations.
- A four-quadrant grid defines service strategies according to operations and (cost) orientations.
- The four quadrants can be referred to as experience management, value-added services, environmental control, and innovative solutions.

....NOTES

1 This chapter is coauthored with Michael Levy and Britt Hackmann. It draws heavily on a white paper entitled, 'The Service Edge in the Retail Marketspace,' by Dhruv Grewal, Michael Levy, and Britt Hackmann.

2 Interview with Laura Sen, former CEO, BJ's; Interview with Steve Germain, former AVP Manager of Analysis at BJ's; Interview with Julie Somers, former VP, Marketing Communications, BJ's Wholesale Club.

3 See: www.zappos.com/about/; Susan M. Heathfield (2017) 'Find Out the Ways Zappos Reinforces its Company Culture,' *The Balance,* 9 September, available at: www.thebalancecareers.com/zappos-company-culture-1918813 (accessed 20 July 2018); Kelly Cheng (2013) 'Zappos: A Case Study in Work Environment Redesign,' *Deloitte University Press,* June, available at: www2.deloitte.com/content/dam/insights/us/articles/zappos/DUP345_Case-Study_Zappos_vFINAL.pdf (accessed 20 July 2018); Jim Edwards (2012) 'Check Out the Insane Lengths Zappos Customer Service Reps Will Go To,' *Business Insider*, available at: www.businessinsider.com/zappos-customer-service-crm-2012-1 (accessed 20 July 2018).

4 Erika Morphy (2009) 'The Bright Spots and Sore Spots of Apple Customer Service,' *Dallas Morning News,* 28 July.

5 Vindu Goel (2016) 'Apple Shifts From Genius Bars to Genius Groves, Hoping Patrons Linger,' *The New York Times*, 19 May, available at: www.nytimes.com/2016/05/20/technology/apple-shifts-from-genius-bars-to-genius-groves-hoping-patrons-linger.html (accessed 23 July 2018); Sam Costello (2018) 'Make an Apple Store Appointment Using the Apple Store App,' *LifeWire*, 7 February, available at: www.lifewire.com/make-apple-store-appointment-with-app-1999600 (accessed 23 July 2018); Rachael Pincus (2015) 'Apple Revamps Its Genius Bar for a Better Customer Experience,' *PSFK*, 23 March, available at: www.psfk.com/2015/03/apple-genius-bar-concierge-service.html (accessed 23 July 2018).

6 Macala Wright (2011) 'How HSN's New Crowdsourcing Project Could Shake Up Online Retail,' available at: https://mashable.com/2011/01/27/hsn-crowdsourced-marketing/#GI9HMuJtVkq3 (accessed 8 August 2018).

7   Bridget McCrea, 'Home Shopping Networks Ramp Up Their Efforts in the Mobile Space as Supporting Companies Jump into the Fray with New Options for Cashing In on Digital Trends' *Response Magazine*.

8   Alicia Fiorletta (2013) 'HSN Transitions to "Boundary-less Retail"' *Retail TouchPoints*, 6 February, available at: www.retailtouchpoints.com/topics/omnichannel-cross-channel-strategies/hsn-transitions-to-boundary-less-retail (accessed 23 July 2018).

9   *India Retail News* (2013) 'CVS Caremark: MinuteClinic Supporting Diabetes Month with Free Diabetes Screenings,' 25 January.

10   Martha Hamilton (2014) 'Walk-in Health Care is a Fast-Growing Profit Center for Retail Chains,' *Washington Post,* 4 April.

11   *India Retail News* (2013) 'CVS Caremark: Innovative New Feature on CVS/Pharmacy Mobile App Helps Users Identify Potential Drug Interactions,' 8 July; *PR Newswire* (2013) 'Aetna Collaborates with CVS Caremark and Dovetail Health to Help Members Manage Their Prescriptions,' 20 August; Stephanie Clifford (2013) 'Stage-Managing Paths to the Prescription Counter,' *The New York Times*, 19 June; William Shrank (2014) 'Engaging with Patients at Pharmacy,' *Drug Store News*, 19 May, p. 48; Antoinette Alexander (2013) 'Pharmacy Advisor Boosts Adherence,' *Drug Store News*, 16 December, p. 30; *PR Newswire* (2013) 'CVS Caremark Uses Data to Combat National Prescription Drug Abuse Epidemic; Program Details Published in New England Journal of Medicine Online,' 22 August.

12   *Chain Drug Review* (2008) 'With Beauty 360, CVS Fashions an Aura of 'Prestige',' 24 November, p. 5; Molly Prior (2009) 'CVS' Beauty 360 Opens Third Store,' *WWD*, 15 May, p. 12; David Pinto (2008) 'Nothing is Beyond CVS' Grasp,' *MMR*, 10 November, p. 8.

13   Hilary Milnes (2016) 'Rent the Runway Snapchats Customers the Right Fit,' *Glossy*, 15 August.

14   Kroger, 'About Kroger,' available at: www.thekrogerco.com/about-kroger (accessed 23 July 2018); Laurianne McLaughlin (2014) 'Kroger Solves Top Customer Issue: Long Lines,' *InformationWeek*, 2 April, available at: www.informationweek.com/strategic-cio/executive-insights-and-innovation/kroger-solves-top-customer-issue-long-lines/d/d-id/1141541?page_number=1 (accessed 23 July 2018); Sandy Skrovan (2017) 'Kroger's Analytics and Personalized Pricing Keep it a Step Ahead of its Competitors,' *Food Dive*, 10 July, available at: www.fooddive.com/news/grocery-krogers-analytics-and-personalized-pricing-keep-it-a-step-ahead-of-its-comp/446685/ (accessed 23 July 2018); CGT Staff (2017) 'Kroger Using Data, Technology to "Restock" for the Future,' *Consumer Goods Technology*, 17 October, available at: https://consumergoods.com/kroger-using-data-technology-restock-future (accessed 23 July 2018); Dan Orlando (2017) 'Kroger CIO: Data Collection is our Present and Future,' *Supermarket News*, 5 May, available at: www.supermarketnews.com/retail-financial/kroger-cio-data-collection-our-present-and-future (accessed 23 July 2018).

15   Interview with Carrie McDermott, COO and EVP, DSW.

16   See: https://corporate.homedepot.com/; The Home Depot (2018) 'Annual Report 2017,' available at: http://ir.homedepot.com/~/media/Files/H/HomeDepot-IR/2018_Proxy_Updates/HD_AR_Soft-Copy.pdf (accessed 23 July 2018).

7

EXPERIENCE: IN-STORE, ACROSS CHANNELS

 Text-specific Definition

What is Experience?

For this book, experience refers to the customer, using a holistic view that spans every response a customer might have to a retailer: emotional, affective, social, physical, cognitive, and so on. It encompasses both factors that are under the retailer's control and elements outside its grasp.

For modern retail firms to survive, the highly competitive environment requires them to go beyond basic pricing and promotion strategies and manage the entire, comprehensive, complete 'customer experience.' But just what is customer experience, and how can retailers manage it? Various retailers have achieved great success in this effort by consistently addressing every single point of contact they have with each customer.

Thus, we start this chapter by offering a definition of customer experience and customer experience management. For the former, we adopt a definition from Verhoef and colleagues: it is

holistic in nature and involv[es] the customer's cognitive, affective, emotional, social and physical responses to the retailer. This experience is created not only by those factors that the retailer can control (e.g., service interface, retail atmosphere, assortment, price), but also by factors outside of the retailer's control (e.g., influence of others, purpose of shopping).'[1]

For the latter, we note that customer experience management is a business strategy designed to produce a win–win value exchange between the retailer and its customers,[2] encompassing the various channels the retailer deploys – including the store itself, as well as mobile and online channels – its assortment and communication decisions, its pricing and promotions, and its attempts to measure the customer experience.

We address each of these aspects of the fourth E, experience, in turn in this chapter, using real-world examples from entrepreneurial retailers, including HSN, Staples, Macy's, CVS, Nordstrom, Victoria's Secret, and BJ's, that integrate multiple channels to make the customer experience more consistent, seamless, and appealing.

These innovative retailers clearly have looked at the overwhelming evidence, whether from researchers or real-world evidence: When customers interact with a retailer across multiple channels, they spend more. They are more likely to return. They grow more loyal. They even appear to spread more positive word of mouth about this retailer, which is there for them whatever channel they choose to follow at a particular point in time.

Thus, an entrepreneurial mindset requires that retailers find ways to encourage their customers to interact with them across multiple channels. But simply getting in-store customers to visit a website (or vice versa) is not sufficient, of course. Instead, the true goal must be the effective integration of the retail offer across channels. Through integration, the retailer achieves greater control over and management of the customer experience. Thus, great retailers, such as HSN, create an interlinked network through which customers can engage with them and experience their content over numerous channels (e.g., on TV, online, on the iPhone, on third-party sites).[3]

A Hypothetical Example

Let's make this point clear with a negative, hypothetical example. A customer named Jean loves visiting the local storefront of SuperRetailer. The store is exciting and engaging, with vibrant colors, streaming music, and bright signage, covered in exclamation points and

Image 7.1
Illustration of
SuperRetailer

dramatic fonts. The clerks are hip and fun, joking around with customers even as they get them through the store and checked out quickly. Although the merchandise is relatively high priced, frequent and specific deals move items out the door rapidly, so Jean feels compelled to buy immediately upon finding something appealing. In addition, SuperRetailer regularly stocks hundreds of items, in a wide variety of colors and sizes, including both manufacturer brands and its own private labels, so there is a lot to choose from in the store. SuperRetailer's private-label brand is cool and exciting, with cutting-edge designs and options, enhancing its fun image.

As Jean was checking out on a recent day, the sales clerk pointed to the bottom of the receipt, on which was printed the website address for SuperRetailer. 'Check it out!' enthused the clerk. 'We just got our website up and running. It's awesome, so visit it the next time you're surfing the web. We're going to get a loyalty program going soon too, so be sure to set up an account, so that you can get all the benefits. Then, next time I see you, I can give you loyalty points for everything you buy!'

Jean is enthused and later that evening, after checking e-mail, pulls out the receipt to head straight to SuperRetailer's site. As it loads, slowly and erratically, Jean finds a brown background on the loading page, with SuperRetailer's name in gray and what looks to be Arial font, and nothing else. Jean waits a few moments for more elements to load, but nothing happens. Looking closely at the bottom of the page, Jean finds small links on the left-hand corner to four options: 'About,' 'Contact,' 'Locations,' and 'Purchase.' The About page provides a textual description – again in gray against the brown background – of the history of SuperRetailer. The Contact page lists the corporate headquarters' office address and an

800-number. On the Locations page, Jean finds an option to put in an address and a link to Google Maps. Finally, the Purchase page provides a static menu of about 50 items. The static pictures feature the offerings on plain white backgrounds. Next to each picture is the name of the item, an item number, and the price. Jean tries clicking on the item name, and nothing happens. Clicking on the picture provides a larger version of the same picture.

Jean is, of course, a bit disappointed. This isn't fun at all! Next, Jean peers more closely at the screen, looking to find something that would lead to the loyalty program sign-up page. Having no luck with this search, Jean clicks back to the homepage, to be able to get back to the Contact page, and calls the 800-number, in the hope of getting some help in this pursuit. Unfortunately, Jean is on the West Coast, and headquarters is on the East Coast, so a recording indicates that the offices are closed and asks callers to call back between the hours of 8:00 a.m. and 5:00 p.m. EST. Jean hangs up and closes the window on her computer, then crumples up the receipt and tosses it in the trashcan. 'Well, that was a waste of a half-hour,' Jean mumbles in frustration.

Integrating Experiences Across Channels

This example is a little obvious, of course. Although in the early days of e-commerce, we might have found such a boring, static, unappealing website, advances in technology and greater experience mean that relatively few modern retailers would offer something quite so awful for their web customers (see Chapter 5). But its point is more broadly instructive. When the value, image, and offerings that a retailer provides in the store fail to match the value, image, and offerings it provides online or through mobile channels, customers end up frustrated and a little disgusted. In our preceding example, Jean not only crumpled her receipt, but she also might have suffered a vastly deflated sense of loyalty, because SuperRetailer ruined her excitement, failed to engage her, and offered virtually no education through its website.

Our retail partners for this book are great; they are no SuperRetailer. That is, their multichannel offerings are closely integrated, from home, to store, to online, to catalog, to mobile. Their assortments are carefully tailored, such that even if the offerings across channels do not match exactly (it can be nearly impossible to maintain all the items available on a website in each local store), the retailer makes it easy for customers to access their desired version. Furthermore, the information that appears in the various channels is not only consistent but extensive. Many of these game-changing retailers even exploit their multiple channels strategically, to ensure that the information available in one place complements and enhances the information available elsewhere. If the retailer chooses to vary prices across channels, it makes it clear why and what elements lead to these price differences. In many cases though, entrepreneurs ensure that the pricing is consistent, wherever the customer encounters a price tag.

After detailing the examples that show how retailers achieve this multichannel integration, we also consider the measurement approaches that game-changing retailers are finding they can adopt and exploit, because of their stellar multichannel strategies and efforts.

The Integrated Experience = Home + Store + Online

Integration across channels goes well beyond just putting similar colors or font styles in the store, in catalogs, and on the website (though such visual consistency can be beneficial). It implies that the multiple channels together seek to enhance the customer's experience by expanding the number of choices available, as well as the vastness of information at customers' fingertips.

Amazon is exploring several innovative ideas that would marry the online shopping experience with a brick-and-mortar presence. Current online customers are wary of purchasing large-ticket items such as furniture and home appliances, so Amazon is considering opening up product showrooms where such items could be viewed and tested in person. Customers then can order the products, either in the store or at home later online, for home delivery. Another innovative store idea would emerge as a sleek, high-tech electronics store, similar to Apple Stores. Electronic Amazon devices such as the new Echo smart home speaker could be displayed and purchased. The company also continues to invest in its physical book stores, having recently opened a fifth location in Chicago.[4]

Macy's offers a close integration of its product and service offerings across channels.[5] For example, it added furniture and mattresses to Macys.com, which enabled customers to shop online even at the moment they might be visiting a store to check out the furniture (e.g., sit in the chair).[6] A furniture shopper wants to visit the store to lie on the mattress options, feel the nap of the fabric, or test the height of the kitchen stools. But relatively few people drive delivery trucks in their daily errands, so getting such bulky items home can create a challenge for customers that disrupts and hinders their overall purchase experience. So the innovative retailer facilitates customers' access to the Macy's website, whether in stores or when they get back home, to enable them to set up delivery options, for exactly the piece of furniture they want. Overall, Macy's enable customers to interact easily with its various

Image 7.2
Amazon is experimenting with brick-and-mortar stores

Source: VDB Photos / Shutterstock.com

channels.[7] By facilitating customers' access to the Macy's website while they are still in the store, the retailer enables them to set up delivery options for exactly the pieces of furniture they want. Although delivery options have long been a service offered by catalog and some brick-and-mortar retailers, integrating the online channel has made this element of the experience even more critical. Furthermore, Macy's pays close attention to its ability to integrate across channels when it makes strategic choices about how to promote its private-label INC brand (as we discussed in Chapter 4).[8]

In these cases, the innovative retailers increase their chances of holding on to the customer, because they never give shoppers the motive or opportunity to go elsewhere to find the items they want. Customers who walk through their doors get the items they want, conveniently, quickly, and without demanding much additional effort by the customer – except maybe answering the door when the delivery arrives.

When CVS purchased the mail-order pharmacy Caremark, it faced a different kind of conflict. Some of its clients – namely, insurance companies – wanted pricing consistent with mail order deliveries. But other clients – namely, consumers and plan members – were more interested in a wider assortment that enabled them to choose the medications they wanted and needed.[9] By integrating its channels, CVS granted its business customers, including insurance companies and corporations that run their own health care plans, greater efficiency and cost savings. But by also offering customers a choice of channels, it supported their preferred experiences. Customers also could view their entire history of prescriptions, with both CVS and Caremark, such that the integration across channels made the often complex and challenging experience of managing various medications easier and far more straightforward. Soon thereafter, it rolled out its mobile application as well, such that patients can get to CVS. com on their phones and order a refill of their prescription, whether to be mailed to their homes or picked up in their local stores.

In addition, market research by CVS showed that patients often fail to take their medications correctly or at the frequency specified by their doctors. Such basic errors seemingly increase when patients lack regular interactions with health care providers, who can remind them of the importance of taking their medications every day (or week or so on). When pharmacists interact directly with the patients, their adherence to their medical plans increase. Therefore, CVS links its in-store, telephone, and online channels by allowing patients to order prescriptions online, calling them if new orders are delayed beyond the point they should be (e.g., a 30-day prescription should be filled about once a month), and encouraging them to come into the store if they have questions. Such integration allows CVS to help patients follow their prescription plans and results in healthier customers.[10]

This integrated experience gives customers everything they might want from a pharmacy: convenience in ordering, easy access to expert advice when needed, a ready summary of patients' own prescription history at their fingertips, and a basic expression of concern about their well-being. Because CVS's sophisticated data management techniques – most of which rely on its popular and widely adopted ExtraCard loyalty program – keep track of customers' activities across all these channels, the retailer can ensure a totally integrated experience. And it can keep customers coming back in the most basic of ways: by making sure they are healthy enough to come back.

The Integrated Assortment

Expanded Selection

An overly simplified recommendation would be to suggest that everything the retailer offers should be available in every single channel it maintains. Customers want flexibility and broad assortments, so that they can be sure to find what they want, exactly when and where they want it. HSN excels at this and strives to provide a seamless experience to their customers.[11]

Yet this recommendation is not only overly simplistic but also unrealistic. A central benefit of e-commerce, as Amazon has shown customers for decades, is that a nearly unlimited number of products and services can be offered up in a central (virtual) location. A retailer that maintains a virtual presence, whether on the web or through mobile applications, would be foolish to limit the offerings to only those items that it stocked in stores.

For example, Victoria's Secret devotes most of its relatively small sales floors (around 1,000 stores, averaging approximately 6,000 sq. ft. each[12]) to bras, panties, and sleepwear. These are the products for which the retail chain is best known, and they are the sort of everyday items that consumers seek to find in stores, ready for them to try on and get a sense of the feel and texture. Fashion experts recommend that women have their bra sizes re-measured once a year (or any time they gain or lose weight). Thus, the stores must have a wide selection of sizes available for shoppers to try on in store. In addition, Victoria's Secret relies on sophisticated data analyses to determine exactly which colors, styles, and sizes to stock in each brick-and-mortar store, to reflect local consumers' preferences.

 **A Little Bit About ...**

Victoria's Secret[13]

Victoria's Secret, along with Pink, Bath and Body Works, La Senza, and Henri Bendel, is owned by L Brands, a firm that got its start in 1963 when the first Limited store opened in Columbus, Ohio. Today L Brands owns more than 3,000 specialty stores, and its brands sell in about 800 franchised locations worldwide, in addition to its e-commerce sites. In 2017, L Brands grossed over $12.6 billion in sales and employed more than 88,000 people. Since L Brands first acquired Victoria's Secret, including its stores and the catalog, in 1982, it has transformed the brand into the

(Continued)

(Continued)

leading retailer of women's intimate apparel. Also in 2017, the Victoria's Secret brand alone earned more than $7.3 billion in net sales through its more than 1,600 brick-and-mortar locations and through its e-commerce site victoriassecret.com.

A key factor of Victoria's Secret's success has been its ability to provide excellent customer experiences, focusing on both customer engagement and customer satisfaction, across various channels. For example, the Victoria's Secret mobile app includes a messaging platform designed to provide instantaneous customer support. Although many companies have started using mobile technology to connect with customers, Victoria's Secret's app is unique in featuring a chat option. With this feature, users can take part in public chats and discuss the latest offerings from the brand. The customizable chats support the inclusion of branded emojis and user photos. In addition, in one of the most exciting components, users receive total access to upcoming Victoria's Secret fashion shows, during which they can even live chat with Victoria's Secret models as they wait backstage. Thus, Victoria's Secret is finding success by uncovering new and innovative ways to engage its customers and build a community.

To ensure it has enough of particular sizes, styles, and colors, the retailer finds that most of its store floors are accounted for. It also leaves little room for other product offerings, such as regular apparel, shoes, or swimwear. Thus, even before the emergence of e-commerce, Victoria's Secret relied heavily on its catalog operations. Early catalogs sought to present a tasteful and sexy image, and soon, they took on nearly 'cultlike status' among consumers. In addition, Victoria's Secret offered 24/7 telephone support, such that buyers could place their orders anytime. Direct mail thus remains a primary channel for the retailer; it currently mails approximately 400 million glossy catalogs, which feature glamorous shots of the infamous Victoria's Secret models. On the models – many of whom have become celebrities through their association with the retailer – the lingerie looks great, and the clothing, sleepwear, and boots also gain a sexy and appealing image.

These expanded product offerings represent an attempt by Victoria's Secret to have significance in various aspects of women's lives, not just under their clothes. A woman who loves the fit of a particular bra is likely to appreciate the styling of a bikini made to similar specifications, so Victoria's Secret strategically added swimwear to its product line. Furthermore, women might trust that the brand that helps them look great in just their underwear can also support their efforts to be fashionable and beautiful in their regular wardrobe. Thus, Victoria's Secret offers tops, jeans, and dresses. As shoes grew increasingly prominent as signals of sex appeal, it also added footwear, slippers, and boots.

Indeed, the product line grew so extensive that even catalogs cannot feature everything the retailer sells. Thus, the e-commerce channel continues to gain in importance. For shoes for example, customers feel perfectly comfortable ordering a new boot without trying them on, because shoe sizes rarely change over a person's lifetime. The differences in the products available across channels make intuitive sense to consumers: mostly undergarments and sleepwear in stores, and then these plus regular clothing and shoes through catalogs and online.

For this company though, the online channel also constitutes another form of integration, because it is the location for many consumers to find the annual and infamous Victoria's Secret Fashion Show. The gala event – some estimates indicated that a recent iteration cost $12 million to put on[14] – is televised live, but just as many people watch the show by streaming it on their computers. The first show, in 1999, attracted so many visitors to the website that it crashed nearly immediately. In resolving the issue and enjoying the press that the crash generated (i.e., it might have seemed like a failure, but it emphasized the vast popularity of the brand!), Victoria's Secret ensured another form of integration, across its catalogs featuring the same models that appear annually on television and the website that combines both versions.

HSN similarly seeks to ensure a strong integration across its televised and e-commerce channels. It averages approximately 50 percent more merchandise available online, compared with the number of products that it features during on-air broadcasts. These expanded

Image 7.3
A Victoria's Secret fashion show integrates with its product offerings, even if the versions in stores are a little less flamboyant

Source: Fashion Stock.com / Shutterstock.com

assortments include not just additional products but also variations on the styles, sizes, and colors featured on HSN's regular programming. In this multichannel strategy, the goal is a seamless transition, such that a viewer checking out the Lancôme Paris beauty show being televised on HSN also can visit HSN.com and continue watching it in real time. This move to the online channel offers additional benefits though, because viewers can learn more about each specific item, leading to increased engagement with the offerings and the retailer.[15]

The primary channels that HSN uses support this seamless assortment strategy, in that the retailer strives to adjust its offerings rapidly to the immediate needs of its customers. When the economy is on a downturn, HSN revises the assortment it features on air, to emphasize more cooking utensils, because it has learned that more people eat at home rather than in restaurants when their discretionary income declines. It also adjusts its offerings seasonally and in accordance with various promotions. For example, with the release of *Oz the Great and Powerful*, HSN initiated a massive programming block of items associated with the Disney film, including an Emerald City crystal ring ($79.95) designed by Heidi Daug, accessories by Steve Madden and Badgley Mischka, a Raven Kauffman Couture Feature Bag ($395), beauty products, and home accessories.[16]

Despite its best efforts to sell out of everything it features on its television shopping channel (in the company president's words, 'we buy to sell out'), with such rapid shifts in inventory, HSN invariably faces overstocks on a few products. Here is where the integration of its e-commerce channel becomes particularly effective: even if HSN's charismatic hosts can't sell everything they offer, the website probably can. By reframing the products as exclusive offerings (e.g., 'Limited numbers still available!' 'New clearance items!' 'Free shipping on clearance items!'), HSN turns overstocks into highly enticing deals for its online consumers. Its strategy ensures that these videos are converted into small (e.g., 30-second) segments, which it posts online, in conjunction with the product being sold.[17]

Another form of integration across the televised and e-commerce channels involves the sale of complementary merchandise. A customer who buys a great sweater by calling in to HSN after seeing it on television will likely receive a cross-buy offer from the order taker, who might suggest a pair of pants that would match beautifully. But if this customer is in a hurry or wants to be able to see the pants first, she can head to the website, find the page for her new sweater (which is easy, using the 'Items Recently Aired' link), and quickly scroll down to see the pants that go so well with it – as well as a matching pair of shoes, a nice handbag, and some earrings that would be perfect.

This integration occurs across all its product lines, not just fashion. A customer clicking on the latest version of Nintendo's PS3 gaming system also sees that HSN has available the game *Red Faction Armageddon* at an excellent price. In this case, the goal might be to facilitate customers' movement, from watching television to visiting the website, to ensure they can find what they want and need. Accordingly, its e-commerce channel has emerged as a key revenue generator, accounting for approximately 30 percent of HSN's sales, at more than $600 million.[18] But some customers want to move in the other direction, so HSN also sends text messages to customers who have signed up to request such prompts. For example, if a shopper simply loves Sam Edelman products, he or she can register with HSN, which then will message that fan in the moments right before those items are about to be featured on the television channel. The customer avoids the risk of missing out on a favorite designer; HSN provides a pleasurable experience that helps the shopper make a desired purchase.[19]

Information

Customers rely on various channels to find various information. Thus, game-changing retailers need to make sure the information they want is available in the most appropriate places, through strategic integration across channels. In particular, consumers use different channels, depending on whether they are searching for information, looking for alternatives, seeking entertainment, or ready to complete a purchase transaction. This section clearly relates closely to Chapter 5, but we consider it worthwhile to address some of these points here as well, to emphasize how integration across multiple channels increases the education of consumers. By granting them the flexibility to find information across different, integrated channels, retailers can contribute to a great customer experience.

We turn again to HSN as an example, because its television channel runs 364 days a year (not on Christmas), 24 hours per day, and 7 days a week. As we noted, many customers start by watching the television channel, then visit HSN.com for additional options or simply to catch up on information that they might have missed, if they tuned in a few minutes late. But the online channel provides additional information too, including video tips. For example, the customer could click cooking classes and access a short class with Wolfgang Puck and get access to the recipe and ingredients.[20] Approximately half of HSN's online sales take place

Image 7.4
Wolfgang Puck may cater the Oscars, but he is also available to teach HSN viewers how to cook

Source: Greg Hernandez

within 72 hours of the moment the item appeared on air, which suggests the purchase process initiated when the customer saw the product for sale on the television channel.

Furthermore, HSN's best customers visit the website a minimum of 18 times per month.[21] These 'best' customers purchase the most from the retailer, seemingly because they have learned that the website provides them with additional, valuable information that might not be readily accessible on the television channel.[22] In this sense, HSN is engaging in precise customer experience management, by ensuring that it provides offerings no other retailer can. As one HSN executive highlights, people watch television because they want to be entertained, not primarily to shop. Therefore, HSN first provides entertaining, engaging content, along with appealing products. But then it also goes a step further, to help consumers learn how to leverage those products to make their lives more fun and enjoyable, whether that means learning how to tie a pretty scarf in a new way or enjoying a boost to their seasonal wardrobe. By enabling consumers to learn new things, HSN becomes a constant contributor to and feature in consumers' everyday lives and experiences.[23]

Integrated Pricing

Let's start this section by making sure that we are clear about what integrated pricing does *not* mean. It does not mean that innovative retailers simply charge the same price for the same items in every market and across every channel. Instead, they seek a consistent, integrated price positioning that makes sense and appeals to customers. For Kroger for example, the integrated price is a good value price but not necessarily the lowest price.[24] Rather than an overly simplified price model that demands the exact same prices across channels – and thus leaves way too much revenue on the table – cutting-edge retailers instead vary their prices, but carefully, strategically, on the basis of extensive research, and in accordance with a wealth of customer, channel, and market data.

Customer

The evidence is everywhere: customers have different levels of prices that they are willing to pay. It gets back to the value proposition we established in Chapter 3. If the assortment is exciting enough, some customers care little about what they pay. In other cases, a thrilling deal makes the difference between the customer buying several versions of an item or nothing at all. To ensure an experience that gets the customer excited and engaged, retailers adopt integrated pricing strategies that appeal to each segment with the price structure that most appeals to them.

Recall, for example, how CVS uses its nearly unparalleled customer data, gathered through its ExtraCard customer loyalty program, to induce specific customers to buy more. Rather than simply offering the same coupons to every shopper, CVS specifies its offers to its most loyal customers. If Chris comes in one day and spends $25 on various toiletries, CVS will send a coupon for $10 off if Chris spends $50 on the next visit. Or it might promise a discount on tissues if Chris uses CVS for the next purchase of allergy medication. By paying attention to the kinds of experiences customers already have with the store, CVS finds ways to encourage them to expand their experience, such as through price breaks.

Two people who visit a local Safeway store – same day, same time, same store – also might find their receipts showing different prices for the same item. Using detailed consumer behavior data collected through its loyalty cards, Safeway offers strictly personalized bargains with a relatively straightforward algorithm: If one consumer buys several of the store's private-label products, such as paper towels and glass cleaner, she will receive a great coupon on the store's private-label dishwashing detergent too. Another customer might receive a coupon for the same item, but if his behavior indicates he is less likely to buy the store brand (because he has purchased name brand paper towels in the past), that coupon will be worth much less. A family that lists many children on their loyalty card information get coupons for larger sizes – especially for products that the kids clamor for in the store, like sugary cereals.[25]

 **A Little Bit About …**

Safeway[26]

Safeway is a US-based food and drug retailer that was first established in 1915 in Idaho. The company provided value with low margins and was able to flourish, such that it grew to a remarkable 750 stores by 1926. The following century, it merged with Albertsons LLC in 2015; the conglomerate also includes Jewel-Osco, Shaw's, ACME Markets, United Supermarkets, Pavilions, Star Market, and more. The resulting grocery giant operates more than 2,200 stores in 35 states and the District of Columbia – approximately 1,300 of which came with the Safeway merger. In addition to the vast number of stores, Safeway brought a range of well-known product banners to the table, including Vons, Randalls, Tom Thumb, and Carr.

Safeway's business model has always been based on providing customers with the best experience possible. It is clearly the guiding principle behind many of the innovations Safeway has pioneered and that have since become commonplace in the market. For example, Safeway was the first grocer to price produce by the pound, add 'sell by' dates to perishables, and provide nutritional labeling. It even accounts for some of the first parking lots. And Safeway continues to lead the way when it comes to customer experiences. In particular, it represents the cutting edge for grocery retailing with its mobile app, which enables customers to shop remotely and then have their groceries delivered within two hours. Furthermore, Safeway remains dedicated to providing the best possible in-store experience to its customers, offering expansive specialty departments and high-quality products.

Customers who visit the deli section in Kroger stores tend to exhibit a greater willingness to pay more, in return for enhanced quality or convenience. Accordingly, the store brand that appears on the deli products at Kroger is the Private Selection line – that is, Kroger's premium, higher-priced, private-label brand.[27] Such offerings clearly are not available in all channels hosted by Kroger, but through its careful analysis of its customers, Kroger knows in which categories and in-store channels it needs to make sure it maintains its high-end private-label offers.

Channel

If people are likely to check across several channels before purchasing an item, an entrepreneurial retailer had better offer the same prices, or else make sure that the services that go along with that item are notably more impressive in the more expensive channel. Staples realizes that – even as prices on technology products keep coming down – few consumers just run in to buy the first all-in-one printer they see. Compared with a few years ago, printers are relatively inexpensive, but a shopper looking for a sturdy, fast, high-quality printer that can produce high-quality presentations, support fax capabilities, and scan documents likely has done a little homework before buying. Maybe the shopper checked external review websites and the issue of *Consumer Reports* that listed the best printers available. Having chosen the exact model he or she wants, a Staples consumer likely visits the website first, to see the price and confirm it is in stock. Then he or she might visit the store to make sure the paper tray is not too wobbly or to measure to make sure the dimensions listed are accurate, so it will be sure to fit on the desk space allotted for the printer. The prices in the store should match the price listed on the website, because this customer is highly likely to remember not just Staples' listed price but also the suggested retail price that *Consumer Reports* listed for the model.

Of course, if Staples can convince in-store shoppers that they are much better off from having received recommendations and advice from store clerks, it might legitimately charge more in that channel. Cutting-edge retailers realize that such convictions are rare today though. Even when stores offer substantially more information, savvy consumers try to find ways to avoid paying for it (i.e., freeriding). Thus, consistent prices are likely a necessity for high-involvement products, for which customers have a firm grasp of the price they expect to find in each and every channel. But Staples recognizes that it can adjust its prices depending on the services that go with the channel in which the customer buys. By doing so strategically, it avoids the problem of customer complaints. For example, it confidently charges more to deliver a heavy case of paper to the customer's office than it does if the customer comes to the store to pick up the necessary product, and in this case, it rarely encounters any issues or complaints.[28]

Furthermore, Staples realizes that few customers likely could offer up an accurate price for, say, a stapler on the spot.[29] Thus, someone who needs a new stapler is unlikely to undergo a review of the same extent as the one we described for the printer. Staples then can offer an inexpensive model for free online, when the customer buys a case of staples. Or it can run an exciting endcap promotion in the store, offering up the brightest colored staplers for a low price, not available online, if customers grab an extra box of staples on their trip around the store.

This sort of price discrimination also appeared in our previous discussion of HSN, which boasts of the clearance deals available on its website, not through its television channel. The trade-off in this case is that customers must be willing to run the risk that the items will sell out, if they want to get the differentiated price. In this sense, the prices remain integrated across channels, because HSN makes it clear what is available when and where and for what price.

Market

Recall how we mentioned that Safeway offered different coupons to two people in the same store for the same item? Well, consumer behavior is not the only determinant it uses to integrate but still differentiate its prices. When Washington suffered massive power outages for example, Safeway sent local customers a wealth of coupons for freezer items, knowing that they likely had to restock. Thus, by paying careful attention to the market itself, cutting-edge retailers can integrate their pricing with the experience consumers are undergoing throughout their lives. Of course, the risk is allegations of price gouging. An entrepreneurial retailer that hopes to maintain a positive image among shoppers wants to *drop* its prices on necessities like bottled water in the wake of a natural disaster, rather than jacking up the costs it charges to people in need.

The In-Store Experience

Have you ever walked into a store and just stood there for a moment, thinking, 'Wow...'? Whether entering a vast, dramatic Nordstrom shoe department for the first time, or making a trek to experience the climbing wall and fishing pond at a Bass Pro Shops store, consumers seek, and game-changing retailers find new ways to provide, breath-taking experiences that bring shoppers flocking back to the stores themselves. We have spent most of this chapter talking about multichannel experiences, and that makes sense. We live in a constantly connected, multichannel world. But innovative retailers also know that in many cases, the experience in the store is what transforms casual shoppers into loyal brand ambassadors. Still, the issue of integration is foremost. Because Staples builds its entire value proposition on making things 'Easy' for customers for example, it works constantly to ensure that their in-store experience is as easy as possible[30] (and simultaneously, Staples seeks to make its website experience straightforward[31]).

Creating a great customer in-store experience demands a recognition of customers' expectations of the store. Because Nordstrom charges high prices and cultivates a high-end image,

Image 7.5
Nordstrom's shoe department can be a thrilling experience when shoppers first encounter it

Source: Carl-Philip Ahlbom

shoppers that visit its stores expect to find sales clerks who are attentive, knowledgeable, and willing to spend hours finding just the right shoes to go with a new suit. As an innovative retailer, Nordstrom works hard to match exactly that expectation.

 **A Little Bit About ...**

Nordstrom[32]

Nordstrom, Inc., has transformed from a small shoe seller in Seattle to the leading fashion specialty retailer that it is today. Its central goal – to help 'customers possess style, not just buy fashion' – has made the chain famous for its excellent customer service. Nordstrom encourages its employees to connect with customers and empowers them to help customers as best as they can. Furthermore, it goes above and beyond by sending thank you cards, offering home deliveries and personal appointments, and issuing personal calls to educate shoppers about upcoming sales. The emphasis on customer service has influenced every aspect of the company, even down to its return policy, which states, 'We handle returns on a case-by-case basis with the ultimate objective of making our customers happy. We stand behind our goods and services and want customers to be satisfied with them. We'll always do our best to take care of customers – our philosophy is to deal with them fairly and reasonably.' For Nordstrom, treating customers fairly and reasonably means that there is no time limit for returns or exchanges and that returns are free. This customer-centric model combined with its impressive assortment has helped make Nordstrom America's favorite retailer for three consecutive years.

At Kroger, shoppers instead anticipate the presence of friendly cashiers who open up new registers when lines get too long. At CVS, shoppers often are pressed for time, so it needs to make sure they can pop in and grab precisely what they need, quickly and efficiently.[33] Across the board, customers want to find the exact merchandise they have been searching for, even if that means (as in the case of Staples) that the store makes it easy for them to find it online. And of course, many shoppers simply refuse to pay full price. For them, the regular, full price is simply a reference or starting point, which they use to gauge the amount of discount they can receive when the retailer offers some sort of discount.[34]

For the brick-and-mortar channels of game-changing retailers though, two elements appear most crucial for enhancing the customer experience: store layouts and the checkout process.

Store Layouts

With the recognition that few customers visit a CVS to browse, the drugstore chain made a design decision for all its stores: they would be low profile. That means that when a customer enters the store, the display racks are low enough that he or she can see all the way to the back and along all sides of the store. Thus, it is easy to locate, get to, and grab whatever the customer needs during that trip, from the pharmacy to greeting cards to candy. To continue enhancing this rapid, convenient experience, CVS plans to add drive-through lanes to as many stores as possible, and it aims to fill every prescription within 15 minutes to ensure that customers do not have lengthy waits for their prescriptions.[35]

Checkout Lines

Does this section seem too obvious for a book on innovative retailing? It isn't, we can assure you. The lines in which customers stand, waiting to give the retailer money for items they want to purchase, in some ways can define the entire purchase situation. We briefly described how Kroger has relied on detailed analytics to define the importance of this aspect of the store environment in Chapter 6. The motivation for such considerations stemmed from what the retailer perceives to be grocery customers' primary goal, namely, to get in, get what they want, and get out of the store, with minimal hassle. When Kroger can avoid forcing shoppers to stand in lines that feel unnecessary and interminable, it also can give them a sense that the retailer appreciates them, the business they offer, and the challenges they face in their busy lives. Along these lines, Kroger has extended the ways customers can check out, moving beyond simple self-checkout lines, to ensure that its self-service kiosks feature the most up-to-date, fastest technology.[36] Thus, customers with small orders can pop in and out of the store rapidly. As we described in Chapter 6, Kroger's data analysis showed that lines were notably long not just in the expected after-work hours but also around 11:30 a.m. With a little more digging, it learned that many mobile workers, whose offices were their trucks or cars, stopped by stores for a quick lunch right before the traditional lunch hour. These shoppers hated having to wait in lines with just a bag of chips and a drink, so Kroger opened more lines but also made self-checkout quick and easy.

By shortening the lines for its checkout registers, Kroger also enhanced the interactions between shoppers and employees. When a checkout clerk is less stressed by the need to ring up lots of customers immediately, she or he is more likely to be a little more pleasant, which in turn makes customers, already in shorter lines, even happier to interact with the friendly, less stressed, helpful employee.[37] Thus, making checkout faster makes the entire in-store experience more enjoyable, because the clerks themselves have a better time of it, without having to interact with frustrated and angry clients. Finally, shorter, faster checkout lines reduce the sense of crowding that often afflicts the front of stores, as people and their carts pile up waiting for a register to open.

But the actual level of speed varies for different game-changing retailers. At Staples, though quick checkout (e.g., less than 3 minutes) certainly is important to customers, it produces diminishing returns beyond that point (e.g., a minute or less).[38]

As if making sure the line is quick and offering various ways to check out were not enough, Kroger did some research to find out just what topics customers prefer to chat about with the checkout clerks scanning their groceries. As we noted in Chapter 6, remarkable numbers of customers, close to 80 percent of them,[39] were straightforward with their preferences: chat about the weather. Kroger does not mandate such conversations by checkout clerks, but it has made a particular effort to train its employees to create a pleasing experience by chatting about general, inoffensive, and pertinent topics.

Conclusion

The cutting-edge, innovative, game-changing retailers of today know that a great part of their job is to make the customer experience a compelling, fun, engaging, informative, and exciting one. Achieving those traits demands a retailer that makes the in-store experience great, but then goes the next step by integrating all its channels into the appeal. Multichannel retailing is nearly a necessity today, and the seamless integration of the customer experience, both within and across channels, is what will set the victors apart.

TAKEAWAYS

- Innovative retailers know that when customers interact with them across multiple channels, they spend more, return, grow more loyal, and even share more positive information about the retailer.
- Thus, entrepreneurial retailers encourage customers to interact with them across multiple channels, by offering authentic, effective integration of the retail offer across channels.
- Channel integration grants the retailer greater control over and management of the customer experience, in the form of an interlinked network through which customers can engage and experience content and the retail offerings.

NOTES

1 Peter C. Verhoef, Katherine N. Lemon, A. Parasuraman, Anne Roggeveen, Michael Tsiros, and Leonard A. Schlesinger (2009) 'Customer Experience Creation: Determinants, Dynamics and Management Strategies,' *Journal of Retailing*, 85(1), pp. 31–41. See p. 32 for quote.

2 Dhruv Grewal, Michael Levy, and V. Kumar (2009) 'Customer Experience Management in Retailing: An Organizing Framework,' *Journal of Retailing*, 85(1), pp. 1–14.

3 Interview with Mindy Grossman, former CEO, HSN.

4 Nick Wingfield (2017) 'Amazon's Ambitions Exposed: Stores for Furniture, Appliances, and More,' *The New York Times*, 25 March.

5 Interview with Karen Houget, CFO, Macy's.

6 Ibid.

7 Ibid.

8 Interview with Adams, Macy's.

9 Interview with Helena Faulkes, Former EVP of CVS Health and President of CVS/pharmacy, CVS.

10 Interview with Dennis Palmer, Former Senior Vice President of Operations, CVS.

11 Interview with Judy Schmeling, former CEO, HSN.

12 See: http://en.wikipedia.org/wiki/Victoria's_Secret#cite_note-Blackwell1997-145.

13 Tiffany Nesbit (2015) 'Text-Based Communication Between Retailer and Customer Includes Branded Emojis, User Photos and Multiple Shades of Pink,' *PSFK*, 20 July, available at: www.psfk.com/2015/07/victorias-secret-launches-chat-feature-in-its-pink-shopping-app.html; Maria Minsker (2015) 'Great Customer Experience Starts with the Right Corporate Culture,' *Destination CRM*, July, available at: www.destinationcrm.com/Articles/Editorial/Magazine-Features/Great-Customer-Experience-Starts-with-the-Right-Corporate-Culture-104761.aspx (accessed 9 August 2018); L Brands, 'About Us,' available at: www.lb.com/our-company/about-us (accessed 9 August 2018); L Brands, 'Victoria's Secret,' available at: www.lb.com/our-brands/victorias-secret (accessed 9 August 2018).

14   Karyn Monget (2011) 'A Look Behind the Curtain,' *Women's Wear Daily*, 8 November.

15   Interview with Bill Brand, Former President and Chief Marketing Officer, HSN.

16   Susan Thurston (2013) 'Movie Buzz for HSN,' *Tampa Bay Times*, 23 February.

17   Interview with Brian Bradley, former EVP Digital Commerce and Advanced Services, HSN.

18   Interview with Grossman, HSN.

19   Interview with Bradley, HSN.

20   Interview with Grossman, HSN.

21   Ibid.

22   Interview with Bradley, HSN.

23   Interview with Brand, HSN.

24   Interview with David Dillon, former CEO, Kroger.

25   Stephanie Clifford (2012) 'Shopper Alert: Price May Drop for You Alone,' *The New York Times*, 9 August.

26   Safeway, 'Our Story,' available at: www.safeway.com/ShopStores/Our-Story. page; Safeway, 'Grocery Delivery,' available at: http://shop.safeway.com/ ecom/home?brandid=1; Albertsons, 'About Us,' available at: www.albertsons. com/our-company/traditions-history/ (accessed 23 July 2018); CBS5 (2015) 'Albertsons and Safeway Hiring Hundreds in Wyoming,' KGWN, 21 July, available at: www.kgwn.tv/home/headlines/Albertsons-and-Safeway-Hiring-Hundreds-in- Wyoming-317809541.html (accessed 23 July 2018).

27   Interview with Linda Severin, former VP of Corporate Brands, Kroger.

28   Interview with Shira Goodman, former EVP HR, Staples.

29   Interview with Donna Rosenberg, Former SVP Corporate Pricing, Staples.

30   Interview with Demos Parneros, former President of Stores-US, Staples.

31   Interview with Jevin Eagl, EVP Merchandising and Marketing, Staples.

32   Nordstrom, 'About Us,' available at: https://shop.nordstrom.com/c/about-us (accessed 23 July 2018); Nordstrom, Inc. (2018) 'Annual Report; Christian Conte (2012) 'Nordstrom Built on Customer Service,' *Jacksonville Business Journal*, 7 September, available at: www.bizjournals.com/jacksonville/print- edition/2012/09/07/nordstrom-built-on-customer-service.html?page=all (accessed 23 July 2018); Andrés Cardenal (2015) 'How America's Favorite Retailer is Crushing the Competition,' *The Motley Fool*, 14 April, available at: www.fool.com/investing/ general/2015/04/14/how-americas-favorite-retailer-is-crushing-the-com.aspx (accessed 23 July 2018).

33   Interview with Palmer, CVS.

34   Interview with Andrew Voelker, Accenture.

35   Interview with Palmer, CVS.

36   Interview with Marnette Perry, Former SVP of Strategic Initiatives and Operations, Kroger.

37   Interview with Dillon, Kroger.

38   Interview with Parneros, Staples.

39   Interview with Marnettee Perry, Senior VP, Kroger.

8

ENGAGED CUSTOMERS ARE LOYAL[1]

 **Text-specific Definition**

What is Engagement?

When customers are engaged, they are also loyal. That means they purchase from, or at least start by considering, the retailer nearly every time they seek a product or service that it provides.

Loyalty programs cannot be expected to make customers loyal. Customers often carry multiple loyalty cards, and retailers of all shapes and sizes – from the corner pizzeria to the largest and most sophisticated chains – offer loyalty programs. Some retailers and service providers believe that if they give customers a coupon or some other financial incentive, it will make them loyal. Pure and simple, this is wishful thinking. A truly loyal customer is one that can't be enticed away to go to a competitor. Because we know that most customers can be lured away, we will highlight some examples of good loyalty programs.

In the past, many retailers gave the same coupons to each and every shopper showing a frequent shopper card at the point of purchase. Customers liked getting lower prices as a result, but the programs treated everyone the same, ignoring an important distinction. There were customers who would only make a purchase at the lower price, whereas others would have made the purchase at the regular price. It also did virtually nothing to reward retailers' best customers or provide *customized* incentives with the objective of increasing purchases per visit, visit frequency, or sales of complementary products. Everyone got the same discounts. Generally, those discounts were the same ones offered by every other competing store, thus doing nothing to build strategic advantage like more effective assortment management or more efficient store operations could. If nothing else, this book has revealed that there are some retailers who do things differently than everyone else. Innovative retailers have rejected the notion of one-size-fits-all loyalty programs as ineffective, inefficient, and perhaps most problematically, unengaging.

In fact, some of these innovative retailers simply refuse to offer loyalty programs at all. Supermarkets such as Publix, Whole Foods, and Trader Joe's accept manufacturers' coupons, but they do not provide customized loyalty programs that require consumers to identify themselves in the checkout line. The Spanish fast-fashion retailer Zara also has no loyalty program. Yet in all these cases, the retailers enjoy a strongly loyal customer base. The methods they use to engage customers have little to do with loyalty rewards. Instead, customers keep coming back to these stores because they enjoy the specific, service-oriented environment provided or access to the niche offerings that are available only in a particular location.[2] We have covered the importance of service strategies and product assortment decisions previously. In this chapter, we focus specifically on the cutting-edge retailers that have chosen to use loyalty programs with a clear commitment to establishing programs that engage consumers uniquely, appropriately, and innovatively.

Our research indicates that the fundamental element of the best loyalty programs is a design that induces customers to shop more frequently and spend more money. They actively move customers up the loyalty ladder, transforming regular shoppers into their best and most profitable customers.

The Promise of Effective Loyalty Programs

Prior to the mid-twentieth century, retailing in the United States was essentially a mom-and-pop affair. Retail operations were run and managed by their owners, and owners knew what

Image 8.1
Inside Trader
Joe's where
the exciting
offerings
encourage
loyalty,
rather than a
conventional
loyalty
program

Source:
Ragesoss /
Wikimedia

their customers wanted. In many cases, the owner–manager purchased merchandise with specific customers in mind, then contacted them when the merchandise arrived. With the rise of chain stores like Sears Roebuck and Company, Montgomery Ward, and Woolworth, as well as department store chains like Macy's and The May Company, size soon overpowered managers' ability to have one-to-one relationships with their customers. Corporate buyers purchased what they thought their major target markets wanted, and stores communicated with a largely undifferentiated promotional mix through mass media.

Image 8.2
Department stores
like Woolworth
once defined
merchandise
assortment
choices

Source: Rob / flickr.
com

The History of Loyalty Programs[3]

Loyalty programs have been around for more than a century. The first one, the S&H Green Stamp Program, was introduced in 1896. The program cultivated customer loyalty by issuing stamps that shoppers could redeem for products when they shopped at participating retailers. It was such a hit that S&H issued more stamps than the US Postal Service! The success of the program spurred others to launch similar loyalty initiatives. One notable entry in this list was the longstanding Betty Crocker Points Program, which lasted from 1931 until Betty Crocker retired its catalog in 2006. The program involved printing point values on boxes of General Mills products that could be cut out and redeemed for products from the Betty Crocker catalog. The next big innovation in loyalty programs occurred in the late 1970s, when American Airlines launched the first frequent flyer program. Today the benefits of loyalty programs have made them a critical aspect of the marketing mix for almost every successful company, whether in consumer or business-to-business markets.

Maybe, despite these changes, customers still appreciate a more personalized touch. Until recently, multi-store retailers were hard pressed to provide it. Even as retailers began collecting mountains of purchasing data – such as those obtained when loyalty program members reveal exactly what they purchase on each shopping visit – they lacked the necessary systems, computing capacity and expertise to reach their best customers with personalized, dedicated offers. Today though, innovative retailers gather intelligence to learn about and match their customers' buying patterns, such that they can make customers feel as if every visit is to a local business. International chains with stores all over the world can make each store feel like home, because they know what their various customers want and are likely to buy, based on their previous purchases or on what similar customers have bought as well.

When done right, loyalty programs provide significant benefits. It is easier and more profitable to increase the share of the wallet of existing customers, rather than to identify and cultivate new ones, because considerable effort is required to get a potential customer to buy the first time. In many cases, it might take as many as 10 new customers to replace a 'best' existing customer.[4] It also takes considerably more effort to keep a new customer interested in returning, entice her to come back more frequently, and spend more each time, whether she shops in stores or online. Loyalty programs that succeed in transforming occasional or sporadic customers into the best customers reap substantial returns. Loyalty programs that are undifferentiated or unengaging instead represent drains on the retailer and need to be revised. For example, noting the disappointing performance of its in-store loyalty programs, along with data that showed that 9 percent of its customers accounted for 46 percent of its sales, Macy's rolled out a streamlined program to encourage even more brand loyalty.[5]

We consider five ways that innovative retailers use loyalty programs to increase the profitability they earn from their loyal, best customers (see Table 8.1).

Table 8.1 The Promise of Loyalty Programs

Promise	Example	Additional Exemplars
Foster Meaningful Conversations with Customers	HSN communicating with customers using multiple vehicles (e.g., TV, web, phone) and using different loyalty tiers to customize offers.	Kroger, DSW
Move Customers up the Loyalty Ladder	DSW using promotional incentives to encourage increased customer purchase frequency and spending.	CVS, Staples, HSN, Sally Beauty
Facilitate Behavior-based Segmentation	CVS using trip-based segmentation to develop replenishment strategies.	Kroger, Macy's
Create Strategic Differentiation	Macy's tailoring assortments for different store locations to better match customer preferences.	BJs
Rewarding Best Customers	Staples offering special prices and products to its best customers.	HSN, BJs

Foster Meaningful Conversations with Customers

A meaningful conversation with a customer historically required a one-on-one interaction in a retail store prior to the use of advanced analytics. With each interaction, the salesperson learned more about what the customer wanted and was able to tailor the offering and sales presentation for that customer. Today, these 'conversations' are based on sales data that are collected through loyalty programs and data from other customer touchpoints (e.g., web transactions, calls to the call center). Using analytics allows retailers to learn about their customers and what incentives will trigger future purchases, and these incentives can be tailored over time to each individual shopper. It doesn't make a difference whether a customer responds to an incentive by making a purchase or decides not to; the retailer learns from that consumer's behavior. Loyalty programs help facilitate a meaningful conversation between a retailer and its customers – one that is mutually rewarding. While purchasing from a particular retailer over time, the customer can be offered incentives that are increasingly more relevant, according to the person's purchase history. The more the customer buys, the more information the retailer has to customize and modify incentives that encourages future purchases over time. This cycle, or conversation, continues over and over. Because loyalty programs enable a retailer to follow its customers' purchase history, it learns what its customers are currently buying, then provides incentives for them to buy more.

The conversation does not have to focus solely on increased buying, however. With loyalty data, innovative retailers can increase the value they offer loyal shoppers by providing them pertinent information, how-to instructions for items they have bought, or details about issues involving customer safety and protection. When Wegmans used its loyalty program to communicate with shoppers about a product recall, the result was a conversation that benefited everyone: the shoppers who avoided eating tainted food and the retailer that enhanced its image as a responsible company.

 **A Little Bit About ...**

Wegmans, Where Loyalty Can Be Life Saving[6]

Wegmans is a US grocery store with more than 90 locations across six states. In recent, independent rankings of the best known and most loved brands, it appeared in some of the highest positions. The first store opened in 1930; the company incorporated in 1931. Wegmans first introduced its Shoppers' Club loyalty program in 1990, and since then, it has become a 'tradition,' according to a Wegmans spokesperson. Wegmans also was one of the first grocery retailers to institute a scannable loyalty card. Wegmans Shoppers' Club adds value for customers in a variety of ways. The program features include daily savings on products throughout the store, access to an award-winning menu magazine, online availability of card and receipts online, and check cashing services. They also hold W-dollars – cash value stored on each shopper's loyalty card that can be used at any Wegmans location. However, the feature that gained perhaps the most attention recently is the product recall notification capability facilitated by Wegmans Shoppers' Club. On multiple occasions, Wegmans has used its loyalty card data to contact customers who bought products that have been recalled. When each recall was announced, Wegmans used data mining technology to identify and call customers who had purchased the problematic products. As the director of community relations noted, being a Shoppers' Club member is a great way to get discounts, but recall incidents show that it is also a powerful communication tool between the company and the customer that even could save some consumers' lives.

The multichannel retailer HSN has many opportunities for conversations with its customers. It can interact with its customers on HSN.com, HSN's television channel, its iPhone application, its YouTube channel, its call center, via e-mail, by direct mail, and through other third-party sites. Offering television broadcasts 24/7, HSN entertains its more than 5 million active customers through its marketing, thus enhancing engagement. As we described in Chapter 6, within an hour of its televised broadcast, the content gets posted to HSN.com, providing access to more than 50,000 videos at any one time. HSN is also one of YouTube's largest content providers and corporate users. Its best customers visit its website about 18 times a month, indicating that these efforts serve to maintain high levels of engagement.[7] Amazingly, HSN enjoys about 25 percent of these customers' total purchases in the specific categories they buy from this retailer.

HSN methodically builds personalized conversations with its customers. Once it identi- fies, say, a good jewelry customer, it provides her with additional information about jewelry she might be interested in and offers her access to these products. By sending her a jewelry guide in the mail that features items that will be coming up for sale in the coming month, it fosters ongoing customer engagement. Not only will she know about the latest jewelry collection being offered, but she also has information about exactly when it is going to be offered. Such information effectively drives future business to HSN's television channel, because the customer knows when she can tune in to see pieces of jewelry she is interested in. Even after a particular jewelry segment has ended, inertia influences customers to stay with the channel as other product categories are featured. Customers are thus introduced to other products that they might not have considered before.

When HSN creates appealing introductions to these other products, it capitalizes on this inertia by encouraging customers to return to HSN.com again, this time for further information about a different product category. Customers thus have engaged in multiple touchpoints with HSN: receiving the jewelry guide through the mail, tuning in to view a spe- cific product demonstration on television, remaining on the channel to watch other content on television, searching for more information on HSN.com, and purchasing after logging on to their account on HSN.com. HSN builds on the insights from these different touchpoints to keep interactions with customers going. Its immediate and most obvious response is to ship the product to the customer, but in addition, HSN classifies this shopper as a multichan- nel customer who enjoys watching demonstrations of products on television and then goes online to find more information and make additional purchases. In turn, HSN can notify the customer of the schedules for other televised broadcasts that might be of interest, such as a Fashion Week segment. It can also attempt to get the shopper to browse the website more thoroughly by offering targeted deals or discounts on related merchandise once she lands on the homepage.

Next, HSN also uses its analytical insights to build customer conversations through excit- ing programming that is entertaining, informative, and engaging. Customers can become experts in their areas of interest and share their thoughts with others. Events like Fashion Week, for example, create excitement in much the same way that the Discovery Channel builds excitement with an event like Shark Week. Cross-functional teams within HSN work with fashion magazines and designers to plan an event. HSN schedules these events nearly every week to foster an ongoing conversation and escalate the customer's level of engage-ment. To facilitate the conversation and seal the deal, HSN uses several incentives, such as a flexible pay program, free shipping, or a great introductory price for a new brand or product. One of its best levers is the 'Today's Special' offer, which appears every night at midnight. Future planning for the category and the brand is based on how unique, specific customers shop for the product thus promoted.[8]

Move Customers Up the Loyalty Ladder

Effective loyalty programs move customers up the loyalty ladder, and by doing so, they help motivate customers to change their purchasing behaviors in ways that increase their profit-ability for the firm. From its loyalty card data, CVS Caremark learns detailed information about what each customer is buying, and the profitability of each item purchased.[9] If a cus-tomer shops relatively infrequently, such as once a month and only to buy prescriptions, it will provide incentives that expire within a week. Alternatively, if another customer buys fre-quently but with a relatively low market basket value (e.g., less than $20 per visit), it provides incentives to increase each visit's purchases to, say, $25. It can also use the information to develop incentives that encourage customers who purchase only national brands to consider purchasing private-label merchandise in other categories.

CVS also uses its loyalty data to identify households that purchase less of a category than expected based on the usage rates of similar households. When it finds this sort of evidence, it quickly provides offers like a 'buy one, get one free' coupon. CVS also attempts to stimulate demand for categories that its data indicate should be in a particular market basket but, for

Image 8.3
The coupons
CVS sends
shoppers are
specific and
unique to each
household

some reason, are not. For example, a detailed analysis might reveal that customers who typically purchase childcare products also purchase green cleaning supplies. CVS then provides special coupons for environmentally friendly detergents, paper towels, or sponges to those who normally buy childcare products without purchasing green cleaning supplies during a given shopping trip.

Many retailers also engage in extensive experimentation to determine which promotional offers are most profitable to different market segments. For example, a particular customer segment at DSW might be divided into two groups for an experiment: The first receives a 'buy one, get one free' offer, while the second group gets a 'buy two at 50 percent off' offer. Although equivalent, they are framed differently, potentially influencing some customer segments to respond more favorably to one over the other. If simply wording an offer in a more appealing manner can influence how customers respond to it, it is in the best interest of the company to employ the more effective one, because it has a direct and positive impact on profitability. Therefore, DSW should use the more profitable promotional offer in the future to appeal to and engage a particular customer segment. It can conduct similar experiments with each of the distinct customer segments it has identified, so that it can devise a varying range of promotional offers to appeal to the different segments and move all these different types of customers up the loyalty ladder.

At Sally Beauty, the first step on this loyalty ladder consists of the customer's e-mail address. When customers enter one of the retailer's 3,000 stores or visit its online sites, they receive an invitation to purchase a $5 membership into its loyalty program, with the promise that they also will get a $5 coupon via e-mail. Thus, the company learns customers' e-mail addresses immediately, enabling it to share information about itself that might engage these shoppers on a more emotional level. Next, it takes a careful look at what the customer buys. If a customer purchases hair dye, that person is likely going to need color-safe conditioner,

Image 8.4
Sally Beauty knows that this consumer will need color-safe shampoo soon and sends a coupon to encourage that purchase

Source: Yakobchuk Viacheslav / Shutterstock.com

perhaps a touch-up tool, and then another box of dye in about six weeks. Therefore, Sally Beauty times special offers and incentives accordingly, sending e-mail messages and coupons at just the moment the customer is likely to be looking to purchase those items. Beyond such immediate information, Sally Beauty works to leverage the data it gathers from its loyalty program to design new offerings that will appeal to the demographics and preferences exhibited by its loyal customers, in line with the benefit that we discuss in the next section. In the Chief Marketing Officer's words, 'We're at a place where everything is driven by the customer and driven by data.'[10]

Facilitate Behavior-Based Segmentation

Considering the level of a customer's loyalty can add another layer of sophistication and complexity to an existing market segmentation classification. Many firms segment their customers on the basis of demographics, such as income, gender, or geography; psychographics such as lifestyles; benefits such as convenience or prestige; or some combination thereof. Although they are helpful, these bases for defining segments can be meaningfully augmented through the identification of loyalty-based segments.

At CVS Caremark, its Extra Care loyalty program provides a differential advantage, by helping customers save money in a way that is both very personal and relevant. The incentives are structured around customer segments, which in turn derive from their expressed needs and buying habits.[11] CVS takes the market basket transactions that its customers conduct in its stores – which means literally billions of transactions – and analyzes the data until it finds consistent intercorrelations among the items. Using such analyses, CVS Caremark has segmented its customer base into 22 groups, reflecting distinct reasons for shopping in its stores and different purchase patterns and market baskets.[12] One of these segments consists of people who shop two to three times a week, spend less than $50 per visit, purchase a combination of health and beauty products and food items, and live in an urban location. This group requires a different assortment and replenishment models than would a segment of suburban consumers who shop at CVS less than once per month, spend around $20 per visit, and mainly purchase health aids or prescription medications.

By factoring 22 different shopping patterns into its assortment and replenishment plan, CVS also can better predict sales for each of the more than 20,000 items it carries, and stock more than 7,000 stores accordingly.[13] Therefore, CVS has taken assortment planning and inventory replenishment to a new level, by integrating customer purchase data that it already has collected from its loyalty program.

Create Strategic Differentiation

If managed correctly, the information derived from loyalty programs can be used to engage customers and develop strategic advantages related to merchandising, services, pricing, promotion, and store operations. Let's start with merchandising. We have previously illustrated how entrepreneurial retailers can increase customer loyalty by offering a unique assortment of national, private, and store brands that customers cannot find at other retailers to gain a strategic competitive advantage (see Chapter 3). To the extent that merchandise can be strategically managed in this manner, it enhances loyalty, because customers know what to expect from the products, like them, and trust them. If a retailer does not provide this merchandise offering, customers might decide to patronize a retailer that does.

Macy's capitalizes on its customer data to offer a compelling mix of merchandise that its customers want. It is easy for a retailer to identify which of its current products customers do and do not want based on past purchase history. The difficult part is determining what customers *might* want to buy if the retailer were to carry a particular product or brand. To address this issue, Macy's developed the My Macy's program, which customizes approximately 15 percent of the assortment to fit the wants of various customers who shop at its 810 stores.

My Macy's works through a combination of strong analytics and good, old-fashioned communications with customers by store personnel. For example, a 25-person team is in charge of analyzing clothing size distributions across stores and regions. At one point, this team of analysts recognized demand for, and thus a prime opportunity to sell, size 11 women's shoes in the Midwestern United States. When Macy's began stocking the larger size and featuring them in the stores, word quickly got out that the department store was 'the place' to find stylish options in larger sizes. As a result, it accrued a new group of loyal customers with larger than average feet, thereby setting itself up to satisfy a long unmet need.[14]

Image 8.5
What distinguishes this coffee shop from all the others?

Source: Pxhere

For coffee chains, differentiation can be challenging, because they sell mostly the same thing. By leveraging loyalty programs, especially those supported by mobile apps, they can evoke greater loyalty among specific groups of customers though – namely, those who are likely to become regulars. Starbucks assesses when each of the users of its app tend to visit its stores, then issues coupons to encourage them to repeat their habits or add new ones. Someone who normally comes on Tuesday mornings thus might receive an inducement to visit Tuesday afternoon, as well as on Friday morning. If a coffee drinker already comes in every morning, Starbucks can identify him or her as a candidate for a food offer, to expand the level of engagement this consumer shows. Peet's Coffee and Caribou Coffee also offer loyalty programs, and their benefits and effective targeting help explain why, in a market environment in which restaurant sales are somewhat stagnant, coffee chains keep growing.[15]

Rewarding Best Customers

Loyalty programs are not designed to treat all customers equally – quite the contrary. They offer special treatment to the customers who are the most loyal. Many multichannel retailers upgrade shipping options for their better customers, then notify and invite them to partake in special offers and events. Other retailers, like Staples, use a more subtle approach. Store managers occasionally call their best customers on the phone, just to maintain a personal connection. The tricky part, however, is knowing when to reveal to other customers what the 'best' customers are getting, and when to keep the differential treatment private from the other customers and competitors. Staples uses price at the point-of-sale (POS) as a strategic differentiator. The best loyalty program customers receive lower prices than 'regular' customers. When a 'best' customer swipes his card or types in his account number online, the POS system automatically re-prices the items in his shopping basket.[16] No one besides Staples and the customer knows – be it the next person in line or a competitor.

At Kohl's, efforts to improve its mobile application to make it the centerpiece of its loyalty program led to remarkable success, including an impressive 800 percent increase in usage of its mobile app following a massive overhaul. During a planning 'rumble,' Kohl's chief digital officer and an interdepartmental team of 30 staffers came to recognize that the retailer's loyalty programs should function primarily through its mobile platform. Accordingly, the mobile app has become the central focus of its loyalty program, rather than an add-on running in parallel with a traditional program. Shoppers no longer need to carry a loyalty card or present printed coupons; instead, the app maintains a record of everything they have bought and the exact rewards they have earned through those purchases.[17]

When consumers return to do a bit more shopping, the app also shows them the prices of items they select, then details exactly how the rewards and discounts they have earned will adjust those prices. Furthermore, Kohl's app provides easy functionality for sharing rewards and shopping lists with others. By making mobile the central platform, Kohl's enables customers to save items in their shopping carts and access them from multiple devices.

Image 8.6
Mobile apps are a centerpiece of retailer loyalty programs

Source: Antonio Guillem / Shutterstock.com

For example, if a teen hopes that her parents will buy her a new pair of jeans that she found at Kohl's while browsing during lunch, she can add it to the shopping cart through her smartphone, then ask her parents to review the item on their tablet later that evening when they get home from work.

The mobile app is central to Kohl's recently improved performance; it experienced sales growth for the first time in years. However, it is not the only factor. In conjunction with renovating its mobile app, Kohl's undertook an organization-wide upgrade, under the umbrella of a 'Greatness Agenda.' It is updating stores, and new merchandising deals are adding popular *Frozen*-themed offerings to its assortment. Thus, by enhancing its product assortment in general, while also offering convenient, effective loyalty rewards, Kohl's has engaged customers, getting them hooked on its offerings.[18]

How Kroger Fulfills the Loyalty Promise

These committed, analytical, innovative retailers have made a strategic decision to invest in their analytical capabilities and leverage their loyalty programs, and the resulting data they accumulate, to the fullest. 'Analytical retailers' have emerged in the modern market, focusing their efforts on bringing all the data feeds together and building sufficient analytical prowess so that appropriate insights can be accessed at every organizational and functional level. With a single-purpose mindset, an organizational commitment, dedicated people, and appropriate technology enables them to engage customers and differentiate themselves from competitors in relation to foundational, strategic marketing mix variables. In this section, we devote substantial space to illustrating these innovative tactics and their successful outcomes as they apply to Kroger, an excellent exemplar of an innovative, analytic retail organization.

Kroger is the largest grocery retailer in the United States, with over $70 billion in sales, and the sixth largest retailer in the world. It first began working with the UK-based consulting firm Dunnhumby in 2001, and the partners developed a joint venture, Dunnhumby USA (rebranded as 84.51°). It works directly with Kroger and takes full responsibility for gathering and assessing the available analytics to drive the grocer's loyalty program, merchandising, store operations, and promotions. It looks at Kroger's loyalty card data and examines customer market baskets for a period and through this analysis it can assess whether the customer is price oriented, whether they like to cook, eat healthy, and so on.[19]

 **A Little Bit About ...**

Dunnhumby USA....to 84.51°[20]

Dunnhumby is the top consumer science company in the world. It partners with different companies, both retailers and brands, to help them better understand their own customers. Dunnhumby also has acquired several companies to enhance its customer insights, such as experts in social marketing, merchandising analytics, and advertising technology. The primary goal of Dunnhumby is to help its partner companies cultivate greater customer loyalty through improved customer understanding. Although originally a European company, with headquarters in the United Kingdom, Dunnhumby USA came to light in 2002, when a team of four scientists traveled to Cincinnati, Ohio, to work with the grocery retailer Kroger, Inc. In 2003 Kroger and Dunnhumby officially formed a joint venture partnership. Then in 2015, Kroger formally purchased Dunnhumby USA and rebranded it as 84.51°, which today represents the analytics arm of the overall company.

Kroger is a forerunner in its ability to analyze customer purchase data to engage customers in meaningful conversations and provide a new kind of personalized experience for its customers. It may not take the form of the traditional mom-and-pop store, but the analysis helps Kroger learn more intimately what its customers want and achieve similar results.

Historically, retailer advertising circulars targeted price-sensitive customers. Retail buyers or category managers vied for space in these circulars, ultimately resulting in featured merchandise categories deemed most important and items within a category representing the best deals. Generally, the best deals were available on lower price/lower margin items, appealing to price-sensitive customers, even though shoppers who focused solely on price often were not the most profitable or loyal customers.

In contrast, Kroger uses its market basket analysis to move customers up the loyalty ladder by creating more effective newspaper circulars. It constantly examines purchase data

Image 8.7
If a customer buys deli meat, are mustard and bread in the shopping basket too?

The answer to those questions helps Kroger determine which products to feature

Source: Mike8411251995 / wikimedia

about featured products in circulars to determine if they drive complementary sales of related products. This analysis identifies which products constitute good potential candidates for inclusion in future circulars. For example, when customers purchase sliced deli turkey, they also might purchase additional deli meats, deli cheese, mustard, mayonnaise, lettuce, tomatoes, and a loaf of fresh bread. If Kroger analyzes its purchase data and finds instead that customers tend to purchase deli turkey but not any of these complementary items on the same trip, then turkey is a poor candidate for inclusion in the circular.

Kroger also integrates its loyalty program data into other marketing efforts to enhance its ability to target specific segments of customers using different versions of its circular. That is, Kroger mails 55 million loyal customer mailings every quarter to its various segments of loyalty card holders. These mailings offer promotions on products that customers normally buy, as well as on products that Kroger predicts they would like based on analyses of what similar customers buy. So for example, if a customer's purchases identify him as a member of a young family because he buys macaroni and cheese, hot dogs, Kellogg's Coco-Krispies, and a lot of animal crackers but not milk, Kroger anticipates he might be willing to buy milk and juice boxes during his regular trips to Kroger, too. Those consumers who do not buy milk or juice boxes at Kroger will be sent store coupons for those items. The combination of data from market baskets and from loyalty programs also can be used to assess the price and promotion elasticities of various items, which then can be employed to develop more appropriate price and promotional models to increase sales or profits.

The loyalty card data also enhance Kroger's ability to develop effective behavior-based segments. A customer's shopping habits and purchase data reveal to the retailer whether that person likes to cook or does not cook, whether the shopper has a baby or a teenager, and whether she lives with a cat or a dog or both. Therefore, Kroger does not need to segment customers solely on the basis of demographics like where they live, their age, or their educational status. Instead, it can aggregate customers into more meaningful segments, based on what they buy. Then Kroger assesses these segments in a variety of ways, depending on the question it seeks to answer with its findings.

At a macro level for example, these behavioral data tell Kroger which items to include in the weekly newspaper circular that it sends to one of its predefined customer segments. At the individual consumer level, it can determine which coupons to e-mail to a shopper who hasn't been in for over a week, even though his prior habits showed that he typically came into the store twice a week on average. When they only use traditional segmentation methods, retailers often develop a dozen or so coupon variations. Instead, Kroger mails literally millions of variations to its over 50 million card holders. Most customers receive a unique set of coupons designed to stimulate their future purchases, whether it involves more of what they are currently purchasing, new products that other similar customers have bought and enjoyed, or more frequent purchases.

 **A Little Bit About ...**

Loyalty at Kroger[21]

The age of technology has presented many companies with immense opportunities, as well as new levels of competition. It is no different in the grocery industry, which is being threatened on multiple fronts. Many customers have shifted their grocery purchases to other sources, such as big box retailers like Target or online retailers like Amazon, that offer online ordering and home delivery of grocery items. In turn, some grocery retailers have suffered already. In contrast, Kroger has taken this chance to find new ways to keep pace. Arguably the most important tactic has been its loyalty program.

Kroger uses the data it collects through its loyalty program to create personalized offers, tailored to the needs of the customer, which encourage each customer to move up his or her own loyalty ladder. For example, as part of the loyalty program, Kroger sends out mailings, personalized to the specific customer. As a vice president of loyalty explains, the mailings 'are like snowflakes, no two are alike.' Kroger puts a substantial emphasis on its most loyal customers in the store too, from choosing its assortment to designing its store layout. For its assortment choices, Kroger prioritizes items that its most loyal customers purchase, above all others. Furthermore, it has adjusted its store layout to match the way its most frequent shoppers shop, so they can quickly and easily get in, around, and then out of the store.

Kroger has been successful using these data to generate insights for undertaking initiatives that strategically differentiate it from its competitors. On an assortment level, Kroger provides a better assortment for its customers by looking for gaps in their market baskets. We previously offered the example of a customer whose profile indicates that she should be buying bread, but for some reason, she isn't (see Chapter 3). If after sending her subsequent bread promotions, she still isn't buying, analysts might deduce that the customer has chosen a gluten-free lifestyle. Therefore, after sending her future promotions for gluten-free products that she does respond to, Kroger concludes that it needs to modify its assortment in this customer's local store to include more gluten-free product options. Kroger's private-label strategy might seek to develop and introduce merchandise that appeals directly to specific and loyal customer segments, a strategy that has led to vast adoption of its store brands among its loyal customers.[22]

Many retailers regularly purchase or receive from their manufacturer partners' information gathered by firms such as IRI Inc. to help them make decisions about what and how much to purchase, in which stores they should stock the items, and how they should promote these chosen products. Retailers also work with and rely on their suppliers, who send category captains into stores to make the same types of decisions and manage the overall categories.

Such data continue to be important to retailers such as Kroger, because they provide insights into the buying patterns of their retail competitors. If another grocery chain appears to be stocking up on prepared chicken wings, celery, and blue cheese dressing, Kroger might anticipate that this competitor is getting ready to make a strong pitch to sports fans in the local area. If a manufacturer starts promoting a new product innovation, Kroger wants to know how the product compares with or will affect the sales of alternative products it offers. It does not lose sight of the ultimate consumer, however, even as it gathers as much information as it can to ensure that it can have customer-centric discussions with its vendors, and to ensure that both Kroger and its vendors are successful (and customers are happy).[23]

Finally, successful loyalty programs reward customers, which is a means of engagement all in itself. In addition to discounts and special offers, Kroger rewards its most loyal customers by designing its product assortment according to their wishes. It gives them exactly what they want. For example, Kroger determines what products to carry, and which ones to remove from store shelves, on the basis of what its most loyal customers purchase.[24] It evaluates each stock keeping unit (SKU) according to its specific profitability, the other products being purchased together with profitable items, and the types of customers who purchase these items.[25] Most retailers only look at SKU profitability, or perhaps examine an item's impact on complementary SKUs, when making assortment reduction decisions. But making assortment decisions more broadly on the basis of whether the most profitable, loyal customers purchase the various items, as Kroger does, is relatively rare and notably innovative. Considering that shelf space is a finite commodity, carrying SKUs that do not appeal to or engage loyal customers means that the retailer is taking space away from those items that its best customers want. The general rule at Kroger is that the retailer will not drop SKUs that are important to its most loyal customers, even if those items might be less profitable.[26] But by continually editing assortments to reflect what their best customers are buying, retailers can maintain a competitive advantage that causes loyal customers to feel as if the local store is 'their store.'[27]

Conclusion

Firms offering loyalty programs should be heartened by recent developments, but also be spurred on to improve those programs to achieve additional benefits. Whereas traditionally, many firms have used their loyalty programs to attract customers with short-term promotional offers such as coupons, these efforts are not likely to engage customers or create long-term loyalty. Through the strategic use of loyalty data, innovative retailers can initiate strategic changes that engage their most loyal customers and keep them coming back for more.

Loyalty programs generally work best when they offer a valued perk to members. Amazon's Prime service offers its members free shipping options. Starbucks' rewards program offers a convenient way to order and pay from a smartphone, then rewards frequent drinkers with a free cup of coffee after they earn a certain number of points. Offering services such as free shipping on online purchases, holiday gift wrapping, and tailoring could potentially help woo customers to make Macy's their first-stop shopping destination and then keep them coming back to spend more.[28]

Despite the examples we have provided in this chapter, there is a sense that even the most cutting-edge, innovative retailers have not achieved the full potential associated with the strategic integration of loyalty program data, analytics, and insights throughout the organization. On this front, innovative retailers have room to grow and are gearing up to achieve loyalty data-based programs that can return successful results that we still have yet to imagine.

TAKEAWAYS

- Loyalty programs might have started by just rewarding customers for each purchase, but innovative retailers seek to engage their customers with specific, detailed, and exciting offerings, matched to each customer's preferences and needs.
- An effective loyalty program must start with a foundation of good customer data. Innovative retailers cannot discover what will engage customers if they do not gather extensive loyalty data.

NOTES

1   This chapter is coauthored with Michael Levy and Britt Hackmann. It draws heavily on Dhruv Grewal, Michael Levy, and Britt Hackmann, 'Making Loyalty Programs Sing,' unpublished working paper, Babson College.

2   Interview with Jose Martinez, former Group Director of Distribution and Operations, Inditex.

3   Max Friend 'The History and Future of Loyalty Programs,' *Media Planet*, available at: www.futureofbusinessandtech.com/business-solutions/the-history-and-future-of-loyalty-programs (accessed 8 August 2018); *Forbes* (2007) 'The Lowdown on Customer Loyalty Programs,' 2 January, available at: http://www.forbes.com/2007/01/02/frequent-flyer-miles-ent-sales-cx_kw_0102whartonloyalty.html (accessed 23 July 2018); Steven Norton (2015) 'The Next Step for the Mobile Wallet? Loyalty Programs,' *The Wall Street Journal*, 26 January, available at: https://blogs.wsj.com/cio/2015/01/26/the-next-step-for-the-mobile-wallet-loyalty-programs/ (accessed 23 July 2018).

4   Interview with Mindy Grossman, former CEO, HSN.

5   Miriam Gottfried (2017) 'A Test of Loyalty at Macy's,' *The Wall Street Journal*, 15 June.

6   See Wegmans, 'Wegmans, "About Us: History",' available at: www.wegmans.com/about-us/company-overview.html (accessed 8 August 2018); Pamela Danziger (2018) 'Why Wegmans Food Markets Get The Love of Customers,' *Forbes*, 3 March, available at: www.forbes.com/sites/pamdanziger/2018/03/03/why-wegmans-food-markets-gets-the-love-of-customers/#105bfcd24ce5 (accessed 23 July 2018); James T. Mulder (2014) 'How Wegmans Used Loyalty Card Data to Telephone Customers Who Bought Recalled Fruit,' *Syracuse.com*, 22 July, available at: www.syracuse.com/news/index.ssf/2014/07/how_wegmans_used_loyalty_care_data_to_telephone_customers_who_bought_recalled_fr.html (accessed 23 July 2018); Tom Tobin (2014) 'How Wegmans, Tops Collect and Use Shoppers' Data,' *Democrat & Chronicle*, 5 September, available at: www.democratandchronicle.com/story/money/business/2014/09/05/wegmans-others-tout-rewards-safety-loyalty-cards/15088377/ (accessed 8 August 2018).

7   Interview with Grossman, HSN.

8   Interview with Bill Brand, former President and Chief Marketing Officer, HSN.

9   Interview with Robert Price, former SVP, Chief Marketing Officer, CVS.

10 Drew Neisser (2017) 'How Sally Beauty Gave its Loyalty Program a Stunning Makeover,' *Advertising Age*, 5 April.

11 Interview with Hetena Faulkes, former EVP of CVS Health and President of CVS/Pharmacy, CVS.

12 Ibid.

13 Ibid.

14 Interview with Julie Greiner, former Chief Merchandise Planning Officer, Macy's Inc.

15 Samantha Bomkamp (2018) 'Your Morning Fix is Fueling Chicago's Coffee Boom,' *Chicago Tribune*, 15 January.

16 Interview with Don LeBlanc, former SVP Retail Marketing, Staples, Inc.

17   Aaron Pressman (2015) 'The Department Store App that Outpaced Uber, Tinder, and Nike,' *Yahoo Finance*, 1 May, available at: https://finance.yahoo.com/news/the-department-store-app-that-outpaced-uber--tinder-and-nike-193431641.html?guccounter=1 (accessed 23 July 2018).

18   Ibid.

19   Interview with Simon Hay, Former CEO, Dunnhumby.

20   Dunnhumby, 'Who We Are,' available at: www.dunnhumby.com/who-we-are (accessed 23 July 2018); 'Dunnhumby USA,' available at: www.dunnhumby.com/unitedstates (accessed 23 July 2018); Tom Davenport (2018) '84.51° Builds a Machine Learning Machine for Kroger,' *Forbes*, 2 April, available at: www.forbes.com/sites/tomdavenport/2018/04/02/84-51-builds-a-machine-learning-machine-for-kroger/#7a81ed8864e1 (accessed 23 July 2018).

21   Elizabeth Holmes (2011) 'Why Pay Full Price?' *The Wall Street Journal*, 5 May, available at: www.wsj.com/articles/SB10001424052748703834804576301221367302288 (accessed 23 July 2018); Candice Choi (2013) 'Kroger Bets Shoppers Will Stay Loyal,' *Yahoo News*, 20 June, available at: www.yahoo.com/news/kroger-bets-shoppers-stay-loyal-160857431.html (accessed 23 July 2018); Sandy Skrovan (2017) 'Kroger's Analytics and Personalized Pricing Keep it a Step Ahead of its Competitors,' *Food Dive*, 10 July, available at: www.fooddive.com/news/grocery--krogers-analytics-and-personalized-pricing-keep-it-a-step-ahead-of-its-comp/446685/ (accessed 23 July 2018); interview with Bill Dankworth, vice president of grocery and DSD, Kroger, Inc.; Interview with Becker, Kroger.

22   Interview with Linda Severin, former Vice President of Corporate Brands, Kroger.

23   Interview with Simon Hay, former CEO, Dunnhumby USA.

24   Interview with Bill Dankworth, former President of Grocery and DSD, Kroger, Inc.

25   Ibid.

26   Interview with Becker, Kroger.

27   Ibid.

28   Gottfried, 'A Test of Loyalty at Macy's'.

9[1]

INNOVATIVE RETAIL ANALYTICS FOR ENGAGEMENT

 **Text-specific Definition**

What are Retail Analytics?

Retail analytics go beyond simple assessments of sales or profits. Innovative retailers leverage every piece of information available, then combine them in an efficient, clear framework, to support their decision making and improve their ability to provide value to customers. These sorts of information continue to expand in number, type, and reach, providing new opportunities for using them to engage customers.

Sometimes innovative retailers come up with inspired new ideas and approaches, seemingly by magic. But more often, necessity is truly the parent of invention, such that the retailers on the cutting edge recognize trends in their environment quickly, then respond to them promptly. To be able to do so, they require strong analytical ability, not only to uncover key trends but also to identify solutions and best responses.

Economies worldwide have experienced massive economic crises and recessionary forces in recent years, prompting various governments to attempt economic stimulus packages, austerity measures, and reduced lending rates. These new economic realities in turn have led to buyers who are much more price conscious, deal conscious, and careful about the purchases on which they are willing to expend their hard-earned income.

Simultaneously, radical advances in modern technology exert similarly powerful effects. For example, effective inventory technology today can not only fulfill orders easily but locate any particular item and distribute it from any location to any other location, in nearly real time.[2] To achieve such real-time methods, retailers need to keep expanding their technology capabilities. In addition, RFID is emerging as a critical resource to support customer relationship management, personalized recommendations, and automatic payments, beyond its promised benefits for inventory tracking. Accordingly, more than half of all retailers in a recent survey indicated that they already had integrated RFID into their operations, suggesting that it is no longer just innovative retailers that are embracing this technology.[3] Innovative approaches also are needed to address mobile technologies, which unavoidably are going to be the primary methods for interacting with consumers, even in stores (see Chapter 5).[4]

Leading retailers have increased their reliance on customer-based analytics in their day-to-day decision making. By paying attention to what advanced analytics can tell them, cutting-edge retailers have come to learn that their customers actively seek deals, consume more private-label offerings, and buy more from discount and club retailers.[5] At the same time, consumers expect more from retailers and their merchandise, and they exhibit limited tolerance for mistakes or poor service levels. With such changes, consumers appear more fickle and less loyal; the retailers that can identify and retain the best customers are those that will succeed in the long term.

A Progression of Retail Analytics

In the past, when retailers drove marketing decisions, they engaged in unilateral decision making, using transaction or market basket data. Thus, they relied on metrics such as sales per square foot, gross mean returns on investments, or returns on invested capital, as well as proxies for customer-oriented measures (e.g., traffic, base conversion rates based on traffic, market basket analyses). But as each generation of innovative retailers steadily moved toward more customer-oriented metrics, they recognized the need to communicate their findings throughout the organization and integrate them into overall key performance indicators.

In turn, the notion of customer-oriented marketing tries to combine retailer-centric data with specific customer information to explicate how retail components work in concert with customer perferences and behavior. Key metrics might include the categories and channels in which customers purchase, customer profitability, the mix of sale- versus full-priced merchandise purchased, online shopping cart and clickstream data, purchase frequency, the monetary value of all purchases, and time since the most recent purchase. The combination of various metrics and data can enable retailers to group customers according to their likelihood of making a purchase, then focus marketing resources where they will make the most impact. In turn, it increases retention among customers who appreciate receiving less frequent but more relevant messages.[6]

Finally, the most recent innovation for retailers entails customer-driven marketing, which integrates customer and transaction data, as well as nontransactional data, to reveal which specific touchpoints engage each specific customer. Integrating data from various sources also helps game-changing retailers develop, maintain, and sustain customer engagement. Thus, in the progression of retail marketing, the most innovative exemplars understand the need for good marketing research and customer-based metrics. But perhaps even more important than the metrics themselves, they recognize the need for a strong capacity to translate data and metrics into insights, using appropriate customer and retailer analytics.

The retail restaurant industry offers a good example of this progression. Restaurateurs once might have tried to keep track of their sales in different seasons or days of the week, but today's data analytics systems collect all the vast information that diners provide with every meal, including the types of food they prefer, with whom they socialize, the time of day they like to eat, how often they eat out rather than at home, and so on. Then these systems offer recommendations for the restaurants to improve their service, such as by ensuring a particular menu item is in stock on the day and time that they can expect consumers to order it. By also integrating information from consumers' social media pages, high-end restaurant managers and hosts can ensure that they recognize diners on sight, and welcome them personally, even if they are not regular customers.

For consumers, such operations offer clear benefits. Being known by restaurant staffers gives consumers a sense of status and feeling of uniqueness. Furthermore, a vegetarian diner would not have to listen to a long list of meat-oriented specials, for example, but instead might receive information about alternative menu options that the chef could create. If the restaurant also uses these data to enhance its operations, consumers likely would enjoy shorter wait times and less chance of popular menu items selling out before they can place their order. For the restaurants, the benefits include reduced operational costs, more streamlined service provision, and increased sales.

But concerns persist even among these benefits. For consumers, these systems entail gathering substantial amounts of data, with few means to opt out of providing that information. If someone makes a reservation and pays with a credit card, the company has a lot of information already, and they can do little to stop a restaurant manager from searching for their name online. Thus, privacy concerns are paramount. For restaurants, in addition to being expensive, the systems could lead to an overreliance on data, undermining the personal touch that often leads to service success. Ultimately, personalized service requires a personal touch, but that touch might become far more effective if it is underlain by advanced retail analytics.[7]

Customer Analytics

Tesco processes its customer data at a rate of around 100 baskets per second, which equals approximately 6 million transactions per day.[8] Each product in the customer's shopping basket offers 45 separate data attributes. Thus, a product might be Tesco's own brand, Bird's Eye, an ethnic recipe, traditional, exotic (e.g., star fruit), or basic (e.g., apple). Customers get filtered by their shopping habits and exactly what they buy. From the products they purchase, the analysis moves on to identify who this customer really is and whether he or she likes to cook, hates to clean, has a baby, or lives in a house filled with pets. Perhaps even more interesting is what tends to be excluded from its analyses: where customers live, their age, or their educational status.

Its finer analysis helps Tesco attract customers into stores on the basis of incentives, whether in the form of promotions or in-store merchandising. A customer who never buys the basics, like bread or milk, must be buying them somewhere else, so Tesco offers great coupons for milk and bread.[9] The precision also means that Tesco mails 9 million different variations of its quarterly Clubcard statements to 13 million card holders.

A Little Bit About …

Tesco[10]

Tesco is a global force, with nearly half a million employees, around 6,500 store locations worldwide, and 2017 sales worth more than 49 billion Euro. Tesco has evolved immensely from the moment it opened its first store in London in 1929. That original store sold only dry goods; by 1958 though, Tesco had already expanded its assortment and opened its first supermarket. A decade later, the first Tesco superstore came onto the scene. This superstore expanded on the offerings already available through the supermarket, to include non-food goods. Starting in 1963, Tesco also maintained an innovative (at the time) promotional loyalty program, in which customers collected stamps, earned through their purchases, that could be exchanged for products.

Tesco has long been a retail innovator, such as its position as the first major retailer in the United Kingdom to launch a range of products under its own healthy eating private label. It is dedicated to continuing to stay on the cutting edge too. Recently it established a new core purpose: to 'make what matters better, together.' This new tagline is designed to reflect its commitment to focusing on more than just functionality. Tesco puts the emphasis on understanding its customers and the needs of employees. This focus on the customer inspired perhaps its greatest innovation: virtual stores. These virtual stores appeared in subways and airports, serving the needs of busy customers on the move. Today, Tesco continues to drive innovation through its Tesco Labs division, which experiments with virtual and augmented reality concepts, connected home products, and mobile applications.

If they combine customer data with transaction data, innovative retailers can achieve even more success in triggering purchases. For example, for online retailers, shopping cart abandonment should prompt the issuance of a contact e-mail and perhaps a special, limited time discount to get the customer to come back and complete the purchase. Furthermore, customized websites and recommendations indicate that the retailer is using its analytics to set itself apart from the pack, such that it can trigger the next interaction.

For example, Expedia analyzes its clickstream data together with its customer transaction data to deliver recommendations and create applicable, compelling travel packages that are interesting and relevant to specific customers. The service retailer's analytics not only enable its analysis of clickstream data combined with customer transaction data but also help it deliver recommendations and packages that are appropriate to each unique customer. The result is a higher level of value and greater customer loyalty to the company.[11]

Yet customer data and analytics alone are not enough. For example, Nordstrom uses its past transactions for target marketing purposes, but it also maintains an extensive database connecting customers' transactions with nontransactional knowledge that sales associates gather from working with the customers in stores: at the point of purchase, what drove a customer to add an accessory? What led another customer to change his mind and decide not to purchase? How well did customers seem to respond to a particular promotion? What sentiments do they express?

A Little Bit About ...

Nordstrom's Analytics[12]

As previously discussed, Nordstrom is one of the leading fashion retailers, known for its outstanding customer service. Nordstrom aims to provide every customer with a personalized experience and uses extensive customer data to achieve this goal. Similar to many other retailers, Nordstrom collects point-of-sale data and

(Continued)

(Continued)

data from its website. In moving beyond that standard, Nordstrom also generates extensive data from its millions of Facebook, Pinterest, and Twitter followers. In addition, its Fashion Rewards Program creates a plethora of customer data. But the beating heart of its innovative techniques and methods is an innovation team, dedicated to finding new ways Nordstrom can better serve its customers through a better, more in-depth integration of full-line stores with digital and mobile technology. To facilitate this integration Nordstrom made several tech-related acquisitions. For example, its acquisition of Bevyup, an integrated mobile app, will help empower the sales associate to offer the best in-store experience. The acquisition of Messageyes will add machine learning skills to its portfolio and thus enable Nordstrom to offer more personalized shopping options.

When it sought to determine how consumers would react to the insertion of digital television displays in its stores, the Scandinavian grocer ICA undertook extended analyses of consumers' reactions – as we described in Chapter 3 – spanning multiple studies conducted in collaboration with the Stockholm School of Economics. After it determined how shoppers in its large stores responded, it repeated the experiments in its small stores, just to make sure it had it customer analytics right. That is, a first series of experiments examined the main effects of digital displays on customers' attention, emotions, attitudes, and behaviors in large stores, while the second round of experiments replicated the first, but in smaller stores.[13]

Retailer Analytics

As the questions that Nordstrom uses indicate, each retailer must ask itself: 'How many touchpoints do we really have with customers, and how many of them are focused on customer engagement?' The game-changing retailers have ready answers for these questions, because they have spent time gathering analytics specific to their offer, customer base, and environment. Increasing the number of customer touchpoints is great, but the real key is prioritizing those data by realizing which touchpoints are most important for future interactions with the customer.

The significance of different touchpoints varies by category, channel, and retailer. For example, depending on the type of retailer, past purchases may be more or less predictive of future purchases. Consider retailers that sell frequently purchased items (e.g., grocery, drug, mass merchandise) compared with those that market items purchased less frequently (e.g., apparel) or larger, infrequent items (e.g., big ticket electronics or appliances). For these latter retailers, nontransactional data may be a more critical source of information, because they are timelier and closer to the customer's next transaction.

Most retailers possess various types of data; the innovative ones use their data better than others do. But every retailer needs to understand the types of data available to them and how to leverage them by increasing touchpoints with a customer and improving their integration. The potential for improvement depends on the type of data collected and the systems in place for both collecting and integrating them. For example, many retailers collect loyalty data but fail to use them to their full potential, leaving vast and accessible room for improvement. This improvement can come about through more integration of the different types of data, by developing appropriate analytical tools and implementing them to address pressing business questions.

Furthermore, learning about customer behavior requires determining each customer's preferences for points of interaction that offer the most value. When the retailer collects data close to the point of purchase, they can take a multitude of forms – social, clickstream, transaction, or customer relationship data to name just a few. Knowing which data to leverage using analytics then is the key to unlocking the next best offers and ensuring customer-driven marketing, including pricing, promotion, assortment, and communication decisions.

Home Depot for example recognizes the complexity of some of its customers' purchasing processes, especially when contractors buy for their own clients or end-customers purchase supplies to provide to the designers and contractors they have hired to do the actual renovation work in their homes. Therefore, it provides a dedicated collaboration platform on the Home Depot website. A contractor can show blueprints electronically to the customer; the customer can review them at his or her convenience, and then click right over to the retail side of homedepot.com to find products to fit the blueprint, as well as highlight some others that might not fit the initial plan. With this information, the contractor can make adjustments or recommendations that are more in tune with the customer's tastes.

Visits to Home Depot stores encourage the continuation of this seamless experience: a design center offers both actual examples of the products and a link, on Home Depot computers, to all options available. Thus, customers can show sales personnel exactly what they want. Sales

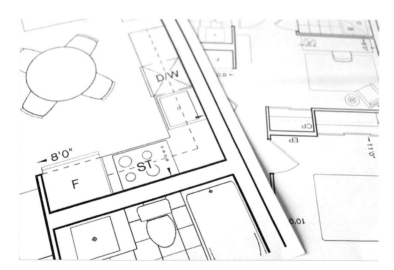

Image 9.1
Home Depot provides a means for contractor customers to share blueprints with their own end consumers

Source: Max Pixel

associates also are armed with mobile devices that support immediate checkouts, display the customer's past purchases, and provide any other details that might facilitate the transaction.

Finally, Home Depot encourages customers in the store to go back online after they leave the store, because then they can continue to evaluate their options as they think about what they need. At every point at which the customer interacts with Home Depot, in stores and online, the combined data collection techniques and related analytics give Home Depot nearly unsurpassed access to high-quality data, right near the point of purchase. Even if customers purchase online, the employee fulfilling the order has the option to contact the customer to ask questions and clarify the buyer's exact needs and wants, such as, 'I'm standing in front of the bay that holds all our front doors, and I see that the version you purchased also comes with a transom window. Are you sure you want the one without the window?'

Strategic Uses of Analytics

HSN perpetually analyzes its viewership data, charting for each televised segment the moment that achieved the highest viewership, then cross-referencing this information with the moment-to-moment sales conversion rates. With this grid, HSN can determine which shows have high viewership but fail to convert watchers into buyers. Thus, it needs to offer more promotions or incentives to get these interested consumers to buy. It also knows that some segments have low viewership rates but great conversion; therefore, it needs to find a way to attract additional viewers, who are likely to buy if they take a look.

Beyond promotional decisions, HSN uses these data strategically to plan its future product mix and refine its scheduling to encourage customers to buy across different categories. Each merchant that partners with HSN agrees to cooperate with the planning group to ensure all data get leveraged and are accurate. Finally, HSN gathers its clickstream data to analyze what makes customers buy in a particular category or a new area, as well as what they are doing on the site, even if they choose not to purchase at all.[14]

All these data imply the need for multiple forms of data and analysis. That is, the data collected and the level of analysis chosen determine how well the retailer can create customer-driven offerings. It needs to adopt a Newtonian philosophy: each action (or interaction) should prompt a reaction. When a customer engages with the retailer, the retailer has to do something about it.

To ensure they are able to do so, innovative retailers ask themselves some combination of the questions shown in Figure 9.1.[15]

Where Are We?

First, innovative retailers should critically and objectively determine where they are overall (the organization's readiness level) when it comes to customer-driven marketing. This effort informs most of the subsequent steps and therefore should be undertaken seriously, carefully,

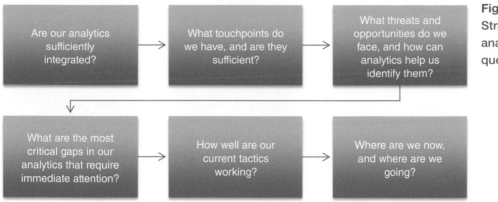

Figure 9.1
Strategic
analytics
questions

and comprehensively. For example, firms need to ask themselves: Do we collect customer data? How much and of what type? How do we use those data once we have them? Are we integrating these data across departments and channels? Is our culture truly customer-centric, or is this customer focus mere lip service? Most retailers have been product-centric for decades, so putting the customer at the center of business decisions requires significant change. It cannot happen without leadership from the very top of the organization, and it requires new capabilities (e.g., data capture, analytic toolkits, skill sets).

As the beauty retailer KICKS came to realize, its growth and the changing needs and demands of its consumer market required it to re-conceive of its approach. Although it had done well in developing its store channel, it lacked a true omni-channel strategy that put the customer first. Through careful analysis of its more than 1.5 million Kicks Club loyalty members, it recognized that to make its online channel function well, it needed to integrate it with the brick-and-mortar stores, because the stores provided the necessary foundation. The cosmetics, hair care, and skincare product markets are plagued by gray and black-market goods, so KICKS made sure to guarantee the brand authorization of every product it sold, through any channel.[16]

A Little Bit About ...

KICKS[17]

KICKS is one of the leading beauty retailers in Scandinavia, with locations across Sweden, Finland, and Norway. The stores carry more than 200 of the top beauty brands, from Lancôme and Dior to MAC and Bare Minerals, in addition

(Continued)

(Continued)

to its own private-label KICKS make-up line. The stores' employees, most of whom are trained make-up artists or beauticians, help give customers the best experience possible, as well as expert recommendations. In a further effort to ensure customers have a totally enjoyable experience purchasing their beauty care needs, KICKS designed its website to offer detailed information about its most recommended products. The website also features helpful beauty guides for each product category, highlighting how to create the trendiest looks with the best, most appropriate, and highest quality products. This form of empowerment enables customers to research what products they need before heading to the store. As another means to empower customers, the Kicks Beauty Award program allows them to review and rank products online. Furthermore, KICKS offers a free, three-tier club membership program. The program includes discounts, newsletters and other mailings, and e-mail and text message offers. A customer can move up through the tiers and earn more benefits by accruing points by shopping more. This program allows KICKS to gain customer data, including purchasing data that helps it provide the best and most valuable deals for its customers.

These customer insights need to be generated in service of action, be understandable, and be consumable by the business functions. Without an honest assessment of their own capabilities, retailers cannot identify what they do well, nor can they find the places they need to improve their methods and tactics.

How Well Are Current Tactics Working?

Second, on the basis of their analysis of their capabilities, retailers should objectively evaluate their current marketing strategies and tactics. Does the marketing department focus on pushing messages about pricing, promotion, and/or assortment to the entire customer base, or does it discriminate effectively? When determining the recipients of marketing communications, do the consideration criteria go beyond recency and frequency scores or recent purchase patterns? Is there a contact management strategy that ensures messages reflect frequency and relevance considerations across all channels?

Because e-mail is such a cost-efficient medium, many retailers fail to consider how an overabundance of such messages can result in customer alienation, rather than the stickiness intended. An untapped opportunity may lie in the organization's ability to leverage its customer insights and marketing practices across channels. When channels operate as separate business units, the organization should honestly assess whether their insights are being shared and marketing communications coordinated in ways that support consistent interactions with each customer, wherever he or she chooses. Integrated customer data from multiple channels can often reveal new and actionable insights into customer preferences and behavioral drivers.

What Are the Most Critical Gaps that Require Immediate Attention?

Third, the gaps from the first steps of this assessment, along with signals evident from customer metrics, can reveal to the retailer where it needs to focus its attention, that is, the issues to prioritize. One firm might perceive that its assortment is great and compelling; it just isn't sure how to induce customers to buy by directing segments to the portions of the assortment that will interest them. Another could feel confident in its promotions, because all its marketing communications prompt customer visits to its website. But this firm also could suffer from high abandonment rates. Yet another may see diminishing response rates or increasing opt-out requests. In each of these cases, the retailer needs to determine the top priority that analytics can help it solve.

For Walgreens, the recognition that customers' top priority was convenience, in all its forms, led the chain to enhance its technology and the related applications. Rather than considering them cold, analytical tools, Walgreens uses its technology to connect more closely with shoppers. For example, for time-pressed consumers, remembering to refill and pick up a prescription can be a stressful, frustrating task. To make this chore more convenient, and accordingly make customers happier and less stressed, Walgreens offers advanced

Image 9.2
Walgreens wants to offer convenience to all its customers, whether in stores or through mobile devices

Source: Rhoda Baer and National Cancer Institute

technology. Customers may sign up to receive text or e-mail reminders to refill a medication, as well as down-to-the-hour reminders to take their prescribed pills. They can scan their refillable prescription label on their smartphones and order a refill in less than 30 seconds, and they can initiate a remote chat with a pharmacist at any time of day. Such technological capabilities actually provide an emotional benefit, such that the shopper feels supported and more closely connected to the drugstore.[18]

What Threats and Opportunities Do We Face?

Fourth, the nature and structure of the data currently available to the firm should exhibit both strengths and weaknesses that in turn define both threats and opportunities. After determining the types of data it has, the retailer needs to start thinking about how to combine them. How do clickstream data complement transaction data for this particular retailer and its unique situation? Are demographic data even needed, or can the retailer halt its efforts to collect them and focus instead on more sophisticated data? Does the combination of customer, transaction, and nontransactional data sufficiently inform the firm's decision making?

If the retailer has extensive, detailed sentiment data, it should recognize their great potential for increasing customer engagement and improving customer relationships. According to evidence that 90 percent of consumers trust peer recommendations but only 14 percent trust advertising, social media are a force that cannot be ignored.[19] When it fails to exploit such opportunities, the firm is left with a lot of data but no sense of what to do with them.

What Touchpoints Do We Have, and are They Sufficient?

Fifth, the touchpoints themselves should undergo analysis, to ensure that they are sufficient in number, appropriate in placement, and focused largely on customer engagement. According to a recently leaked memo, Apple has determined that it should seek to interact with new adoptees of its Apple Watch through the website, rather than in stores. Doing so ensured that they would receive their new products as promptly as possible, thus encouraging greater sales. Even if they come in to the stores, consumers will likely receive a suggestion that they place their orders on Apple's website.[20]

For other retailers, such as those that still rely primarily on a one-way, 'push' mode of communication, the first step likely should be to develop descriptive analytics. With these methods, it can improve messaging related to areas in which specific customers have shown activity or interest and stop sending messages about aspects in which they have no apparent interest.

Sixth, and in a related sense, the analysis of the data infrastructure should reveal points that remain for getting in touch with customers. Perhaps there is an opportunity to add touchpoints to engage the customer, just prior to the purchase event, or to move up the purchase event. If such openings exist, the retailer must realize that it will have a hard time making full use of the data it has, and it likely cannot design the best marketing mix to induce a purchase event.

Even Amazon, with its remarkable reach, can find new touchpoints. A recently unearthed patent application shows that Amazon has plans for a linked system, featuring RFID, facial recognition, and tracking software, that would enable customers to walk into a store, take what they want, and receive a bill for the items they take without ever moving through a queue or checkout line. The software system seemingly would use multiple sources to identify each customer accurately. It also might support an expansion of the lending economy, such that shoppers could borrow some items for some period of time, then return them and pay only for the time they had the items in their possession. This innovation comes quick on the heels of Amazon's first brick-and-mortar store, which has opened on the campus of Purdue University and which enables students to pick up their online purchases, as well as drop off their returns.[21]

For most firms, this gap implies a capability to apply predictive analytics. A gap at another touchpoint might be less critical but still worthy of consideration by the firm, such that it can leverage a descriptive analytic competency it already possesses.

Are Our Analytics Sufficiently Integrated?

Seventh, integration relates to the analysis process as well. In particular, retailers should ensure that their marketing, merchandising, pricing, and other teams are working closely together, using the same combined data, to appeal appropriately to customers and ensure their complete engagement with the firm. Customer insights need to inform decision makers outside marketing, or else the marketing function will be limited in its ability to transform itself to be customer driven.

Even the most innovative retailer is unlikely to emerge from this self-assessment completely satisfied with its efforts. In the new normal, the norm is constant change. As we have explained in this chapter, customers continually shift their approaches, preferences, and desires. Thus, retailers must keep up by continually analyzing their customers, their data, and their analytics. In so doing, they become customer driven, in the true sense of the term, which should support their long-term goal of retail innovation, survival, and success.

TAKEAWAYS

- Modern retail analytics offer innovative retailers more detailed insights than ever before – as long as those retailers leverage the data thus produced in meaningful ways.
- To perform a strategic analysis that creates a framework for using retail analytics, retailers can ask themselves a series of six questions:
  - Where are we?
  - How well are current tactics working?
  - What are the most critical gaps that require immediate attention?
  - What threats and opportunities do we face?

o   What touchpoints do we have, and are they sufficient?

o   Are our analytics sufficiently integrated?

NOTES

1   This chapter benefits from a working paper that was largely based on this book material. The working paper is by Dhruv Grewal, Mary Delk, Matt McNaghten, and Britt Hackmann and entitled 'Transforming Retail: Customer-Driven Analytical Marketing.'

2   Dan Berthiaume (2015) 'TechBytes: Five Hot Tech Trends from NRF 2015,' *Chain Store Age*, 20 January.

3   Dan Alaimo (2015) 'RFID Use Reaching a "Tipping Point",' *Retail Wire*, 30 March.

4   Berthiaume, 'TechBytes'.

5   Yu Ma, Kusum L. Ailawadi, Dinesh Gauri, and Dhruv Grewal (2011) 'An Empirical Investigation of the Impact of Gasoline Prices on Grocery Shopping Behavior,' *Journal of Marketing*, 75 (March), pp. 18–35.

6   Matt McNaghten and Clark Passino (2011) 'Understanding Customer Retention in the Retail Industry,' *Deloitte*, available at: www.scribd.com/document/73841513/Understanding-Customer-Retention (accessed 25 July 2018).

7   Karen Stabiner (2017) 'To Survive in Tough Times, Restaurants Turn to Data-Mining,' *The Wall Street Journal*, 25 August.

8   Tesco (2009) 'Tesco Doubles Customer Rewards in Further Boost to Clubcard,' press release, 14 August.

9   Jenny Davey (2009) 'Every Little Bit of Data Helps Tesco Rule Retail,' *TimesOnline.com*, 4 October, available at: www.thetimes.co.uk/article/every-little-bit-of-data-helps-tesco-rule-retail-6pdh8zg0w9x (accessed 25 July 2018).

10   Tesco PLC, 'Core Purposes and Values,' available at: www.tescoplc.com/index.asp?pageid=10 (accessed 25 July 2018); Tesco PLC, 'Key Facts,' available at: www.tescoplc.com/about-us/key-facts/ (accessed 25 July 2018); Tesco PLC, 'History,' available at: www.tescoplc.com/index.asp?pageid=11 (accessed 25 July 2018); Eddie Wrenn (2012) 'The End of Coming Home to an Empty Fridge: Tesco Opens "Virtual Shop" Inside Gatwick so You Can Stock Up While Waiting for Your Plane,' *The Daily Mail*, 8 August, available at: www.dailymail.co.uk/sciencetech/article-2185336/Tesco-opens-virtual-shop-inside-Gatwick-fridge-wait-plane.html (accessed 25 July 2018); *Designboom* (2011) 'Tesco Virtual Supermarket in a Subway Station,' 6 July, available at: www.designboom.com/technology/tesco-virtual-supermarket-in-a-subway-station/ (accessed 25 July 2018); Bernard Marr (2016) 'Big Data at Tesco: Real Time Analytics at the UK Grocery Retail Giant,' Forbes, 17 November.

11   SAS (2011) 'SAS' "Big Analytics" Tackles Big Data, Speeds Problem Solving,' press release, 12 July.

12   Walter Leob (2018) 'Nordstrom Leads With Fashion, Service and Innovation,' *Forbes*, 12 March, available at: www.forbes.com/sites/walterloeb/2018/03/12/nordstrom-leads-with-fashion-service-and-innovation/#70a306a57f7d (accessed 25 July 2018); Kurt Schlosser (2017) 'In Latest Digital Initiative, Nordstrom Names Longtime Exec to Lead New Innovation Team,' *Geek Wire*, 9 January, available at: www.geekwire.com/2017/latest-digital-initiative-nordstrom-names-longtime-exec-lead-new-innovation-team/ (accessed 25 July 2018); Mark van Rijmenam (2013) 'How Fashion Retailer Nordstrom Drives Innovation With Big Data Experiments,' *Datafloq*, 22 August, available at: https://datafloq.com/read/how-fashion-retailer-nordstrom-drives-with-innovat/398 (accessed 8 August 2018).

13   Krista Hill, Anne Roggeveen, Dhruv Grewal, and Jens Nordfält (2014) 'ICA: Changing the Supermarket Business, One Screen at a Time,' Babson Case Study, 1 December.

14   Interview with various senior leaders at HSN.

15   The section draws on the unpublished working paper by Dhruv Grewal, Mary Delk, Matt McNaghten and Britt Hackmann and entitled 'Transforming Retail: Customer-Driven Analytical Marketing.'

16   Pontuz Bjelfman and Nanna Hedlund 'This Is KICKS', *KICKS*.pdf, 2014 Shopper Marketing and Pricing Conference, Stockholm School of Economics.

17   See: www.kicks.fi (accessed 25 July 2018); Facebook, 'About KICKS,' available at: www.facebook.com/kicks/info?tab=page_info (accessed 25 July 2018); Axel Johnson AB 'KICKS,' available at: www.axeljohnson.se/en/koncernbolag/axstores-2/ (accessed 25 July 2018).

18   Bridget Brennan (2015) 'Convenience Can Be Emotional: Lessons from Walgreens CMO Sona Chawla,' *Forbes*, 7 April.

19   Erik Qualman (2011) 'Social Media Revolution,' Social Media video series.

20   Matthew Stern (2015) 'Apple to Push Customers from its Stores to its Site,' *Retail Wire*, 10 April.

21   Matthew Stern (2015) 'Could Amazon's Brick-and-Mortar Invention Eliminate Checkout Lines?' *Retail Wire*, 3 April.

10

CONCLUDING THOUGHTS

This book has presented a lot of ideas about what constitutes innovative, game-changing retailing. The examples span a range of fields – from department stores to e-commerce, drug stores to grocery, and a plethora of specialty retailers – and the related implications are vast and varied. Therefore, to help readers get a handle on what they can do to enhance their own status as retail innovators, we have proposed a five-factor framework, which we call the 5 Es. In this, our last chapter, we review what this framework consists of, what it means for retailers, and how it helps all of us move forward into the future of retailing.

As a reminder, the 5 Es are:

- Entrepreneurship
- Excitement
- Education
- Experience
- Engagement

We discuss each of these 5 Es in turn. In each of the following sections, we use a single example of an innovative retailer, though as the preceding chapters have shown, there are multiple examples to demonstrate each of these 5 Es. That is, there is no single right way to achieve entrepreneurship, excitement, education, experience, and engagement. Nor does any single retailer represent the very best example across the board. Rather, we attempt to highlight some well-supported, well-known exemplars, in the hope of inspiring new innovative retailers to pursue this challenging and rewarding path.

Figure 10.1
The 5 Es

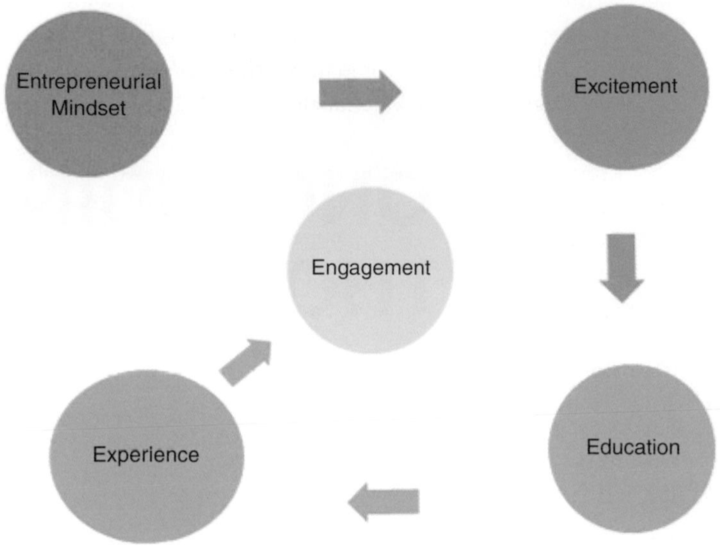

Entrepreneurial Mindset

Understanding entrepreneurship requires understanding how people with creative ideas transform into entrepreneurs who lead an organization to greatness. As we discussed in Chapter 2, these entrepreneurial leaders often take the road less travelled. Our focus is not on traditional theories of leadership, which are widely available elsewhere. Rather, we address how any entrepreneurial leader can produce innovative retail, by following five clear principles. Remember what they are?

1   Keep the strategy simple.
2   But make sure it is well developed too.
3   Then keep the execution of the strategy consistent...
4   By integrating it across all firm elements, and
5   Ensure that it is communicated to all audiences.

As an example of keeping it simple, we described how Kroger adjusted effectively to changing customer and consumer needs by maintaining its existing, well-defined strategy but altering how it applied that strategy. Thus, Kroger persisted in its simple strategic goal of earning customer loyalty for life, but it adjusted what that goal meant, and what actions it required, when it recognized how dynamic demographic shifts were leading new customers, or existing customers with new needs, to visit its stores.

This simple strategic goal and its implementation derived from Kroger's careful assessment and analysis of its particular portion of the retail sector. As the grocery sector changed, so did

Kroger, according to a well-developed and precise understanding of both itself and its surroundings. This innovative retailer persists in its extensive marketing research, in partnership with Dunnhumby, and thus is able to weather whatever changes come its way – a recession, a recovery, the growth of private labels, expanded online shopping, shifting demographics, and so forth.

Such consistent dedication to the development of a simple strategy provides another benefit too, in that it helps the innovative retailer execute its strategy consistently, across the entire firm, and in a way that is clear to customers, employees, suppliers, managers, and other audiences. When Kroger says that it will earn customer loyalty for life, it makes that effort a key part of its very brand image. All departments, from the top management level to temporary employees, are encouraged to embrace the notion that their purpose is to earn this loyalty for life. Encouraging such an embrace across the entire firm requires clear communications, because everyone needs to be on the same page in terms of comprehending the strategy (which, again, is possible because the strategy is simple and well-developed). Kroger thus constantly trains employees to put customers first, communicates to customers that it considers them first, requires suppliers to help it put customers first, and maintains a top management dedication to putting customers first, even if the innovative, entrepreneurial leaders that helped it achieve this status might change.

Excitement

To be honest, we think just about everything involved in innovative retailing is inherently exciting. But in the chapters dedicated to this second E in our framework, we focus particularly on two key elements: how exciting merchandise creates value for innovative retailers and how exciting store brands offer compelling benefits for innovative retailers and their customers.

Merchandise is exciting when it features the right items, available at the right place and time, at the right price, for the right customers. Accordingly, in Chapter 3 we propose a three-part definition of exciting value, comprised of what, when/where, and how elements. These aspects might be familiar, in that they often appear in traditional descriptions of retailing too. But the way in which innovative retailers apply and adopt these three notions set them apart from the pack.

The 'what' involves merchandise selection, additions, retention, and deletions. An innovative retailer applies its entrepreneurial strategy to find just the right balance – enough merchandise to attract shoppers, not so much that it creates confusion or frustration. For example, CVS works with suppliers to maintain a collaborative planning, forecasting, and replenishment system that helps it minimize the threat of out-of-stock situations. This system also helped it take the innovative step of defining what customers wanted, such that the retailer was able to reduce its inventory levels but simultaneously increase its in-stock levels.

When CVS considers adding a new product to the 'what' it carries, it makes sure to assess the option carefully. For example, using an innovative testing approach, it loaded a new display in a few stores with both existing and newly introduced pain relief products, then determined how customers responded. A similar procedure helps CVS delist certain items, whether across the chain or just in certain stores. Perhaps the most notable and widely covered example was CVS's choice to stop carrying any tobacco products. Through a careful and innovative review of what customers valued, as well as what brought value into their purchasing patterns, CVS took the radical and unprecedented step among drugstore chains (though one that is already being copied) of deciding that it could and should stop selling the unhealthy, damaging products throughout the nation.

This example refers to a chain-wide decision, but innovative retailers also take care to adopt merchandise strategies that account for 'where' and 'when' questions. Thus, CVS removed cigarettes from all its stores. But it also determined that, unlike suburban customers who drove to the drug store, shoppers living in city settings needed to be able to grab convenient sizes of regular grocery items, like milk and coffee. Therefore, it adjusted its assortments to reflect this 'where' aspect. In urban settings, most CVS stores look a little something like a general store, carrying a bit of everything for everyone. However, in more suburban locations, especially if the store locates next to a hardware store in the same strip mall, for example, the CVS is less likely to carry items like light bulbs. Instead, it bulks up its inventory of health-related and fun items that shoppers are unlikely to find at any other outposts in the same immediate vicinity.

The 'when' and 'where' questions also apply within each individual store, as innovative retailers make strategic and well-developed choices to allocate their merchandise inside their stores. Innovative retailers are experimenting with all sorts of clever options for getting customers excited. From the innovative displays that CVS uses, as we described just previously, to high-tech signage and creative seasonal promotions, the retailers at the cutting edge get customers excited about walking through their stores, ready to be thrilled by what awaits them in the next aisle.

Finally, the 'how' questions revolve around two key elements of any retail interaction: pricing and promotions. Here again, CVS is at the front line of innovation. Its ExtraCare and myWeeklyAd efforts were among the first to leverage the vast power of customer data. Depending on how customers have shopped previously, CVS determines what types of promotions to offer on the next visit. The promotions can vary in the products offered, sizes involved, price discounts offered, type of discount (e.g., buy-one-get-one, dollars off, percentage off if total bill exceeds a certain amount), and so forth. In addition, the myWeeklyAd circular is totally personalized, offering each customer a flyer that reflects his or her past purchasing habits and likely interests. This online promotion even allows shoppers to develop personal shopping lists, then tells them on which aisle they can find their desired purchases in their local store.

Such personalization and dedicated offers are greatly appealing to customers – so much so that many innovative retailers have taken the next step and started to provoke excitement about store brands, dedicated to the specific needs of customers who patronize those particular stores. Store brands create excitement in five main ways: by enhancing the assortment, through branding, through differentiation, by expanding management potential, and through identification. As we detail in Chapter 4, for innovative retailers, store brands are thus equal parts exciting and challenging. But when the retailer does it right, they are just plain exciting for the most important member of the supply chain, the customer.

In this context, HSN offers a stellar and cutting-edge example. As it continues to grow, this innovative retailer has expanded its assortment dramatically, such that shoppers can access tons of products: clothing and accessories, housewares and kitchen appliances, cosmetics and skin care, jewelry and shoes. In addition, in its varied collaborations, whether with relatively unknown innovators or globally famous celebrities, HSN gives customers an assortment of options and associations, limited only by their own preferences. Whether amateur gourmands love Wolfgang Puck or Jamie Oliver, they can find products that match their preferences among HSN's held brands.

With these subbrands, the company also reinforces its image as a fun spot to find a little bit of everything. Because in many cases shoppers also can find those items only on HSN, the retailer achieves superlative differentiation – 'only on HSN' will a customer get excited at the prospect of finding Nikki Minaj chatting with callers. Of course, because such experiences are possible only on HSN, it also faces some notable challenges, because its brand is behind every store-branded item it sells. As an innovative retailer though, HSN has a simple and well-developed strategy in place to address these challenges: 'We plan every minute of every day,' as an executive we interviewed explained. With its unique approach, HSN literally documents sales in every channel during every hour of the day, then makes adjustments as necessary to ensure that customers are finding exciting value. Because they do, customers identify closely with the retailer, its brands, its store brands, and the excitement that these combined elements bring to them.

Education

In traditional retailing theory, educating customers involves making them aware of the products on offer – their features, availability, prices, and so forth. Innovative retailers still need to engage in that sort of education, but they do not stop there. Rather, education today takes place at the intersection of new forms of media, including social, mobile, and online. It also focuses increasingly on service education and the ways in which cutting-edge retailers can provide innovative solutions to all customers' needs.

In Chapter 5, we talk about social media and the education that comes with it. This education goes both ways: innovative retailers rely on social media to listen to what their customers are saying, analyze what they want, and then do what is required. In addition, by maintaining a constant and consistent presence, in accordance with their simple and well-developed strategy, that spans all these channels, innovative retailers make sure their customers take them into consideration. That is, they guarantee that customers are educated enough at least to think about visiting their stores, their websites, their mobile site, their app, or their social media page.

The listen–analyze–do framework resonates with these forms of education, in that it details how innovative retailers can be educated by, even as they are educating, their customers.

For example, the modern version of Macy's is one that is listening all the time. Whether on external social media sites such as Twitter or on its own webpages, Macy's maintains constant vigilance, looking for feedback, complaints, or concerns. In addition to responding promptly to all customer comments, the cutting-edge retailer logs the comments, such that it can determine trends or broad demands. It also gathers visit frequency data, people's stated style preferences, and the motives they list for visiting a store, online channel, or social media page. That's all part of the analyze step. Finally, it makes sure to take these lessons to heart and do those things that will appeal to consumers. For example, with the data it gathers, Macy's can determine a relatively precise likelihood that any particular customer will spend some particular amount in a particular merchandise category. With that information, it can leverage its various resources to help the customer find what he or she wants and encourage a purchase that benefits both the shopper and the retailer.

Because a strong education is a foundation for new innovation, Chapter 5 winds up with some examples of truly futuristic experiments being conducted today and potential innovations in the future. From item-level RFID scanning to smart dressing rooms to clothing that tells wearers what shoes will match, Macy's and other cutting-edge retailers remain at the head of the pack, promising continued retail innovations.

Some of these innovations are likely to continue leveraging the service education that we discuss in Chapter 6. For that discussion, we propose a four-quadrant categorization, defined by current versus new operations and revenue-generation or cost-containment goals. The interactions of these spectra of approaches to innovative retail lead to four types of service strategies that retailers can use to educate customers. Thus, in this summary, we diverge a little from the pattern in the rest of this chapter and offer retail examples of each of the four types.

First, when retailers focus on experience management, they seek to use their current operations to generate revenues. For example, BJ's Wholesale Clubs does not need to radically change its operations when it works to educate its customers that they can find smaller or single-service products, along with the large, value packs it is best known for, on its store shelves. With such educational initiatives though, BJ's might increase the revenues it earns from current and prospective customers, using the same operations and strategy. Second, if they shoot to provide value-added services, innovative retailers pursue new operations that can earn them more revenues. With its value-added service strategy, Staples has expanded its service offerings. Once, people just visited the office supply stores to pick up toner and paper; today, it helps customers create complex, professional-looking print jobs and brochures, in a simple and straightforward way. This expansion accordingly generates revenue for the innovative retailer.

Third, a retailer that adopts store environmental control maintains its current operations and also seeks to contain its costs. At Home Depot for example, the home improvement retailer implemented new, user-friendly inventory control systems. In so doing, it lowered the risk of shelf stockouts (e.g., when merchandise stays in the stockroom, even though the shelf is empty, because no one knows the items are available in inventory) and also enabled employees to help customers more quickly and professionally (i.e., because the system tells them on exactly which aisle to find each item). These improvements did not entail a radical change in the retailer's operations, but they led to diminished costs and happier customers. Fourth and finally, innovative solutions arise when a retailer investigates new operations while also trying to cut costs. These solutions can probably best be exemplified by the expanding array of self-service technologies offered by retailers. As long as customers enjoy and appreciate the possibilities of such game-changing innovations – such as touch-screen menus at fast service restaurants like Buffalo Wild Wings and Chuck E. Cheese – they can alter the cost structure involved in serving and educating consumers.

Experience

Of the various elements that constitute a retail experience, in Chapter 7 we highlight those that ensure an integrated and enjoyable interaction between an innovative retailer and its customers. Integration involves several facets, including across channels, across assortments, across prices, and – even in our modern, technologically dependent world – in stores them-selves. An innovative retailer cannot ignore the simple notion that retail shopping should be an experience that customers want to repeat, over and over again.

For example, whether consumers experience Victoria's Secret by entering a store, brows-ing the catalog, clicking online, or watching a fashion show on television, they should come away with a similar, integrated perception. All these channels are vastly different – stores maintain a relatively small selection, and the fashion shows have no purchase options, for example – and yet they provide a similar experience. The items available for purchase are luxurious but still mostly accessible. The color scheme relies heavily on pink tones. The image is sexy but still generally tasteful, and the celebrity models on the runway are the same ones featured in the catalogs.

Engagement

There are so many loyalty programs today, and they span so many industries, that it might be easy to forget just how innovative they were when they first were introduced. We offer, in Chapter 8, a brief history of loyalty programs and how they have functioned to enhance, expand, and illuminate customer engagement. Through well-run loyalty programs (which differ from undeveloped, one-size-fits-all approaches), innovative retailers get the chance to enter into meaningful conversations with customers, often going deeper than the initial listening they might be doing through their social media links with customers. They also can engage customers more deeply with the retailer, encouraging greater purchases or more frequent visits. Similarly, loyalty programs reiterate and emphasize a strong retailer's differen-tiation from its competitors. A good loyalty program also informs the retailer about optimal segmentation methods, based on customers' actual behaviors. Finally, to be engaging, a loy-alty program must make sure to reward the retailer's best customers.

For example, with its loyalty program, the shoe retailer DSW determines whether shoppers would prefer a 'buy one, get one' promotion or a promise that they can 'buy two at 50% off.' The price differences are minimal, but the outcomes for both the retailer and the shopper diverge notably. When a customer signals a preference for one promotion or the other, DSW knows how to reward him or her, adds another piece to its segmentation calculations, and has a clear way to encourage continued purchases.

As we also note in this chapter, a loyalty program holds little real promise if it is not backed up by powerful analytics. That is, to be truly innovative and engaging, a retailer also needs to be analytical. With a strong analytics capability, a retailer can apply the education it has gleaned, the excitement it has wrought, and the experiences it has participated in to define its entrepreneurial strategy at every level of the organization.

We consider analytics so critical to innovative retailing that we continue this discussion in Chapter 9. In this context, analytics can refer to customers or to the retailer itself. Combining all the different types supports a strategic use of the information, which in turn can initiate a self-sustaining, virtuous cycle of retail innovation. To get it started, we provide six questions that innovative retailers, and retailers that hope to become more innovative, can and should ask themselves:

1   Where are we now, and where are we going?
2   How well are our current tactics working?
3   What are the most critical gaps in our analytics that require immediate attention?
4   What threats and opportunities do we face, and how can analytics help us identify them?
5   What touchpoints do we have with customers, and are they sufficient?
6   Are our analytics sufficiently integrated?

That first question is something all of us must consider at all times, of course. But for innovative retailers, the answers to these questions are vast and varied. To answer them, innovative retailers must begin with an entrepreneurial mindset, established and encouraged from top to bottom. With this foundation, they can manage to generate excitement throughout the market, providing value and benefits to both their own firms and the customers they serve. Asking such questions also is fundamental to the pursuit of education – again, both for the firm and their customers. Answering the questions will help innovative retailers create an experience that shoppers enjoy and hope to repeat, which can set the stage for closely engaged, loyal customers.

As the future of retail unfolds, new technologies, market developments, and customer trends will require realignments and reconfigurations of what constitutes the cutting edge in this industry. But the 5E concept we have proposed herein should continue to apply. Even if someday robot retail employees deliver virtual reality services to space-age shoppers, the ones that do it best will be the ones that know how to excite, educate, and engage consumers with entrepreneurial experiences.

INDEX